Harvard University
Center for International Affairs

REFLECTIONS ON THE FAILURE
OF THE
FIRST WEST INDIAN FEDERATION

By Hugh W. Springer

OCCASIONAL PAPERS IN INTERNATIONAL AFFAIRS

Number 4

JULY 1962

AMS PRESS
NEW YORK

Harvard University
Center for International Affairs

ABOUT THE AUTHOR

Hugh W. Springer, C.B.E., M.A. (Oxon), and Barrister-at-Law of the Inner Temple, is a West Indian educator, writer, and sometime politician, Barbados-born and Oxford-educated. He has been Registrar and chief administrative officer of the University College of the West Indies, at Kingston, Jamaica, ever since it was founded in 1947. Before this he was a lawyer and political leader in Barbados, serving seven years in the Barbados House of Assembly and three on the Executive Council. For more than twenty years he has been active in various public affairs; for example, in the 1940's he was General Secretary of both the Barbados Workers Union and the Barbados Labor Party, and in recent years he has been a member of the West Indian Trade and Tariffs Commission.

Mr. Springer wrote this Occasional Paper in the spring of 1962 while he was a Fellow of the Center for International Affairs, Harvard University.

OCCASIONAL PAPERS IN INTERNATIONAL AFFAIRS

Number 4

July 1962

REFLECTIONS ON THE FAILURE

OF THE

FIRST WEST INDIAN FEDERATION

By Hugh W. Springer

Published by the
Center for International Affairs
Harvard University
Cambridge, Mass.
1962

Library of Congress Cataloging in Publication Data

Springer, Hugh W
    Reflections on the failure of the First West
Indian Federation.

    Original ed. issued as no. 4 of Occasional
papers in international affairs.
    1. West Indies, British--Politics and government.
I. Title. II. Series: Harvard University.
Center for International Affairs. Occasional
papers in international affairs, no. 4.
[F2134.S6 1973]   320.9'729   70-38762
ISBN 0-404-54604-8

Reprinted from the edition of 1962, Cambridge
First AMS edition published in 1973
Manufactured in the United States of America

AMS PRESS INC.
NEW YORK, N. Y.   10003

On September 19, 1961, the people of Jamaica by a majority of 54 to 46 percent decided to withdraw from the Federation of the West Indies. Four months later the ruling party in Trinidad, fresh from a resounding victory at a general election, passed a resolution to the effect that Trinidad should not take part in a Federation of the Eastern Caribbean. On May 31, 1962, almost exactly four years after the inauguration of the Federal Parliament, the Federation of the West Indies came to the end of its legal existence.

The purpose of this essay is to record the writer's reflections on the failure of the Federation and what he conceives to be the causes of this failure. These reflections are contained mainly in Chapters 3 and 4. The first two chapters give an account of the growth of federalism in the West Indies and describe the way in which the Federation came to its untimely end. The fifth chapter discusses the prospects for the future, partly in an attempt to justify the writer's optimism and buttress his wishful thinking.

Hugh W. Springer

CONTENTS

REFLECTIONS ON THE FAILURE
OF THE
FIRST WEST INDIAN FEDERATION

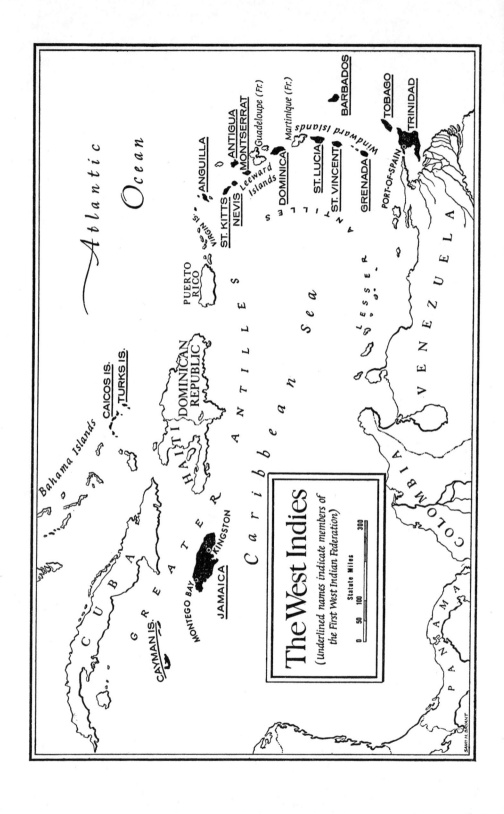

The West Indies

(Underlined names indicate members of
the First West Indian Federation)

Statute Miles

0   50   100   300

Atlantic

Ocean

Atlantic

ANGUILLA

ANTIGUA

MONTSERRAT

Guadeloupe (Fr.)

Martinique (Fr.)

BARBADOS

TOBAGO

TRINIDAD

ST. KITTS

NEVIS

Leeward Islands

DOMINICA

ST. LUCIA

ST. VINCENT

GRENADA

Windward Islands

PORT-OF-SPAIN

VIRGIN IS.

Leeward Islands

PUERTO RICO

A N T I L L E S

L E S S E R

Caribbean Sea

VENEZUELA

COLOMBIA

P A N A M A

CAICOS IS.

TURKS IS.

DOMINICAN REPUBLIC

HAITI

Bahama Islands

C U B A

G R E A T E R

A N T I L L E S

CAYMAN IS.

MONTEGO BAY

JAMAICA

KINGSTON

SAM H. BRYANT

CHAPTER 1

THE GROWTH OF FEDERALISM IN
THE WEST INDIES

I.

The idea of federalism has been abroad in the West Indies for a long time. From the earliest days of settlement in the seventeenth century, the idea of uniting two or more islands for administrative convenience or economy has appealed to the British Government, but there has been little unification in practice. Governors have frequently been shared, as until very recently one was shared by Grenada, St. Lucia, St. Vincent, and Dominica (the Windward Islands) and another by Antigua, St. Kitts-Nevis-Anguilla, and Montserrat (the Leeward Islands). Barbados has at different times in the past shared its Governor with other islands of the Lesser Antilles, and the Governor of Jamaica was for a time Governor also of British Honduras. The Leeward Islands had a federal government of a sort, which lasted from 1871 until 1957, when the Federal Government of the West Indies was about to be inaugurated. The attempt to join Barbados in a federal union with the Windward Islands in the 1870's, shortly after the Leeward Islands Federation had been created, was defeated by violent local opposition which culminated in the so-called confederation riots in 1876.

After this failure the British Government attempted no more federal experiments in the West Indies for seventy years—until the end of the Second World War. The federal idea continued, however, to have irresistible attraction for British Colonial civil servants acquainted with the West Indies; and a number of them at various times put forward schemes for closer union and federation of these islands, usually in articles in British journals and in speeches to interested audiences in Britain.

[1]

The idea continued to be popular also with visiting commissions, until the turn of the century when a degree of reserve became noticeable. The Royal Commission of 1882–83[1] (whose assignment was to inquire into the financial conditions, with a view to the more economical administration, of Jamaica, the Leeward Islands, the Windward Islands, and Tobago) recommended the closer association of all the British territories in the Caribbean, with a federal union as the ultimate goal. Again in 1894 a Royal Commissioner,[2] sent to Dominica to inquire into the affairs of that island, went out of his way to recommend an administrative union of all the British Antilles under one Governor General. The Royal Commission of 1896-97[3] used a more cautious approach; while recommending the improvement of communications between the islands, it limited their unification proposals to Barbados and the Windward Islands. Major Wood[4] (later Lord Halifax), who in 1921, as Under Secretary of State for the Colonies, came to investigate the political development of the territories, was equally cautious. He thought that public opinion was not yet ready for federation, and that communications were not good enough to make it practicable. He suggested that the possibility of joining Trinidad with the Windward Islands should be explored.

The other pre-World War II commissions were even more reserved. The Closer Union Commission of 1932–33 (which like its predecessor of 1882–83 had been prompted by the need for economy) rejected anything politically closer than the sharing of one governor by the Leewards and the Windwards, while the Royal Commission of 1938–39, which came to inquire into the causes of the recent wave of disturbances, strikes, and riots, expressed the view that the time was not ripe for federation. This commission did not, however, reject the idea. On the contrary, they questioned the witnesses who came before them in a political capacity and recorded that: "Almost every witness thus questioned was in favour of closer union." They themselves concluded

1. Cmd 3840/1884. See also L. E. Braithwaite, "Progress towards Federation," *Social and Economic Studies,* University College of the West Indies, June 1957.
2. Cmd 7917/1894.
3. Cmd 8655/1898.
4. Cmd 1679/1922.

that "the combination into one political entity of all the British possessions in the area is the ideal to which policy should be directed," and recommended that "an attempt should be made to overcome local prejudice against Federation, both by exposition of its theoretical advantages and by testing these in practice through the amalgamation of some of the smaller units."[5]

II.

Among West Indians themselves there was not much talk about federation until the period between the wars. The West Indian leader whose name was chiefly associated with the idea of federalism during this period was Albert Marryshow (later Senator Marryshow), a member of the Legislative Council of Grenada and founder-editor of the newspaper *The West Indian.* He was a well known figure and widely traveled in the eastern Caribbean. He even visited Jamaica—a rare accomplishment in those days. But his influence was virtually confined to the eastern part of the region. There it played an important part in giving a West Indian slant and purpose to the political agitation for reform of the Crown Colony system in the direction of self-government, which had already begun to make itself felt in the press and from public platforms.

This was the time when the labor movement, which had begun uncertainly in Trinidad and British Guiana at the turn of the century, was showing signs of vigor under Arthur Cipriani and Hubert Crichlow in those territories and under Duncan O'Neil in Barbados. Except in British Guiana, trade unionism was still untried. For the time being, the distinction between political reform and economic betterment was blurred, and popular leaders agitated for constitutional change and social justice with equal fervor and in the same breath. Their main targets for attack were their different local governments and ruling classes, but the target they all had in common was the Colonial Office, which represented the ultimate source of constitutional reform, and which at that time was by no means as accessible to popular leaders as it subsequently became after they had acquired political power. It was natural that the popular

5. Cmd 6607/1945, p. 327.

[3]

leaders of the territories in the eastern Caribbean should come together to discuss their common problems and to formulate united courses of action. Inevitably the question of union (and in the West Indian circumstances inevitably federal union) came to the forefront of their thinking and was readily accepted as a remedy for their divided weakness.

An important stage in the progress of the federal idea in West Indian thinking was marked by the conference in 1932 at which a group of liberal and radical politicians from Trinidad, Barbados, the Windward Islands and the Leeward Islands, meeting in Dominica, decided that West Indian federation was desirable and in the general interest, and drafted outlines for a constitution. They presented these proposals to the Closer Union Commission of 1932–33, who, as we have seen, rejected them on the ground that public opinion was not yet ripe for federation. This commission had been appointed by Lord Passfield in pursuance of the request of the elected members of the Executive and Legislative Councils of Antigua that, as a measure of economy, the Windward Islands and the Leeward Islands be united with Trinidad under one government. The West Indies, like the rest of the world at that time, was feeling the effects of the economic depression of the 1930's.

The depression brought to maturity the growing working-class movement. Between 1934 and 1939 a succession of disturbances, strikes, and riots (see Appendix A) erupted along the British Caribbean chain from British Guiana to Jamaica; and out of these emerged a numerically strong and militant labor movement. The leaders of the movement in the southernmost territories (the Windward Islands, Barbados, Trinidad, and British Guiana), loosely associated under the title of the West Indies and British Guiana Labor Congress, held conferences in 1938 in Trinidad and in 1944 in British Guiana, at which they passed resolutions in favor of federation of the West Indian territories. The 1938 conference adopted a constitution for the proposed federation drafted by Grantley Adams[6] (afterwards Sir Grantley), who later became successively the first Premier of Barbados and the first Prime Minister of the West Indies.

6. Ebenezer Duncan, a legislator of St. Vincent, also drafted a federal constitution for the West Indies that was published in 1944.

[4]

In September 1945 a notable expansion was achieved by this unifying movement of West Indian labor leaders, when a conference held in Barbados was attended by delegates not only from the southern territories, but also from the Leeward Islands and Jamaica, and indeed from as far north as Bermuda. At this conference the Caribbean Labor Congress (CLC) was founded, with a constitution and officers and a secretariat. The conference also passed a number of resolutions on federation as well as on West Indian development.

This conference brought together a remarkable constellation of West Indian leaders. Some of them, like A. A. Thorne and Hubert Crichlow of British Guiana, had been active since the beginning of the century and had already achieved their greatest successes. Others had come to the fore and achieved distinction in the years following the First World War. Of this group, Albert Marryshow was outstanding and was at this time at the height of his prestige and influence. Arthur Cipriani of Trinidad would have been his rival as the most distinguished political figure, but he had died a few months before. A third group of men whose stars were rising included Grantley Adams of Barbados, Albert Gomes of Trinidad, Norman Manley of Jamaica, and Vere Bird of Antigua. Adams was the best known and most successful of them, Gomes was aspiring to the place vacated by Cipriani, Bird was about to win control of the Government of Antigua, and Manley had recently lost the first round of the political contest in Jamaica to his rival Bustamante.

Manley was unable to be present at the conference, but his party (the People's National Party) was represented by a member of its executive, who was mandated to advocate a strong federation which would be able to unify and so strengthen the weak and vulnerable economies of the separate colonies. He brought a letter from Manley, the following quotation from which indicates the manner in which the prospect of federation was then regarded by those in Jamaica who had thought about the question:

> We of the West Indies are now, I firmly believe, developing a firm understanding of the necessity of hammering out and holding to common outlooks and jointly strengthened courses of action. Certainly we of the Progressive

Movements in Jamaica have stepped right out of the old frame-work in which we saw our problems, so far as we saw them at all, in isolation and as affecting ourselves alone. I think we can give a solid assurance of adherence to a West Indian outlook.

It is inevitable that the problems of Peace will concentrate a great deal of the energies and attention of each element in the West Indies on its problems and it is a misfortune that during the war when the forces of cohesion might most easily have developed the limitations of transport denied us access to each other. As the war years recede so it will become harder and harder to build the foundations of new structures requiring unity for their success.

This present Conference meets at a unique time of opportunity and it is the hope of us all in Jamaica that it will be able to move surely through the difficulties that are bound to arise and end with the establishment of a basis for further action both able to carry the growth of our mutual aims and to withstand the stresses and strains that may develop.

On behalf of the People's National Party and of the Progressive Forces in Jamaica I express our confidence in the work you are engaged in and in the outcome thereof. I feel certain that the new spirit which is alive in the West Indies today will be strengthened and guided by the results of your work and that a foundation will be laid upon which the national life of each Country may with greater sureness and more speedily be built to the end that we may all by our united efforts achieve the full status to which we aspire.[7]

Manley proved to be right in saying that as the war years receded it would become harder and harder to build the foundations of new structures requiring unity for their success. The war had drawn the West Indian colonies much closer together than they had ever been before. The war situation provided opportunities for united action at many levels, and promoted too

7. Caribbean Labor Congress, Official Report of conference held at Barbados September 17–27, 1945, pp. 36-37.

[6]

the expansion of transport facilities which is obviously necessary for the unifying of islands so widely separated from one another. The Colonial Development and Welfare Organization and the Anglo-American Caribbean Commission (later to become the Caribbean Commission and finally the Caribbean Organization) played their part in the process by providing opportunities for conferences and common action. The habit of planning development on a regional basis began in the war years and led to a greatly increased consciousness of belonging together.

III.

This West Indian consciousness reached its peak of emotional fervor in September 1947 at Kingston and at Montego Bay. At Kingston the Caribbean Labor Congress held its second and (as it proved) final conference, at which the leaders of the labor movements in all the British Caribbean colonies reaffirmed their belief in federation and submitted their views, together with a draft constitution,[8] to the Montego Bay Conference which followed immediately. At Montego Bay the official representatives of the West Indian governments (including a number of those who had been attending the CLC Conference at Kingston) met with the Secretary of State for the Colonies, Arthur Creech Jones. They agreed in principle on federal union, and appointed committees to submit proposals for a constitution and to report on other aspects of the process of federation. The speeches of the delegates, with few exceptions, reached a high point of common feeling. Even Alexander Bustamante (afterwards Sir Alexander), at that time head of the Jamaica Government, though not a member of the CLC and not previously committed to federation, expressed himself in favor of it, provided it was adequately financed.

Norman Manley, who was present as a member of the Caribbean Commission, made an eloquent statement of the case for West Indian federation. He paid a tribute to the Colonial Office which had, he said, "for decades regarded the Caribbean territory as one area suffering from common disabilities and requiring in the close relationship between its economic circum-

8. Conference on the Closer Association of the British West Indian Colonies, Part I, Colonial 218 (London, 1948), pp. 121-131.

[7]

stances a generalised policy . . . such as the federal government would build for itself." He emphasized that federations were born of necessity, and out of planning for real needs. "It is impossible," he said, "to suppose that every single one of these territories, or perhaps even the largest of us, can achieve alone the basic services which it is the whole aim of politics to create and make possible for the common man." He reassured those who were afraid that the necessary financial resources would not be forthcoming, and those who were afraid of going forward too fast. He warned against the "vested interest of ambition in power," and appealed to "men who were unwilling to give up any local root of power for the creation of a larger centre of power" to "drop out of their minds their own security, real or apparent, and the years of power and position in their own lands, and see that this larger objective opens our horizons and gives a wider opportunity for all." He expressed his "deep and passionate belief that our areas are destined for nationhood and destined to make a real contribution to the civilization of the world," and concluded with the following peroration:

> I say, here are we all on a sea of world conditions, stormy and hazardous in the extreme, each huddled in some little craft of our own. Some hardly have oars and only a few have accomplished a rudimentary sail to take them along. And here offered us is a boat, substantial, capable of being made sea-worthy and ready to be manned by our own captains and our own crew. If we won't leave our little boats and get into that larger vessel which is able to carry us to the goal of our ambitions then I say without hesitation that we are damned and purblind and history will condemn us. [9]

IV.

The period between 1947 and 1956 was a period of conferences and committees, reports and resolutions, leading to the agreement to federate of February 23, 1956. It was a period during which enthusiasm for the federal idea diminished from the high pitch of 1947 to the level of mere acceptance of the

9. *Ibid.*, Part II, pp. 57-62.

decision that there was to be a federal center. This was the case everywhere except in Trinidad. Here a new figure came into prominence on the political scene in 1956—Eric Williams, leader of the newly formed People's National Movement (PNM), which in one political campaign swept not only into parliament but into power. Williams entered the ranks of the federalists with a fresh approach, and thought it worth while to justify the federal case by argument.

"Federation," he said, "is a simple matter of common sense. The organisation of the British Caribbean territories dates from the seventeenth and eighteenth centuries . . . the age of small countries and small states." He pointed to Germany with "as many states as there were days in the year"; Switzerland, "a collection of cantons and independent cities"; Italy, "a geographical expression"; England and Scotland, with difficulty united in 1707.

In this context it was a mark of progress for Barbados to aspire to be a free state, as was said in 1651, and it was possible for Nevis to request in 1667 to be separated from the government of Barbados on the ground that the Barbadian planters viewed with jealousy the development of the sugar industry in Nevis and wanted to restrain it. A Jamaican proposal a few years later for a joint expedition to put down piracy in the Leeward Islands was rejected by the Barbadian planters with the statement that they would not spend a shilling to save the Leeward Islands.

But we no longer live in the eighteenth century. The first proposals for British Caribbean Federation followed logically from two important consequences of the industrial revolution and large scale production in the nineteenth century. The first was the growth of large central governments— the unification of Germany, the unification of Italy, the attempt of Bonaparte to set up a world empire, the Civil War in the United States to prevent the division of the country into two parts, the federation of Australia and Canada, the growth of the ideal of Pan Americanism. The second was the improvement in methods of transportation and communication—internally by the railway, externally by the steamship and telegraph.

[9]

These trends to larger units of government have become even more pronounced in the twentieth century. Look around the world today and try to find a community of 700,000 people of the size of Trinidad and Tobago playing any important part in world affairs. There is none. There can be none. The units of government are getting larger and larger. Whether federation is more costly or less costly, whether federation is more efficient or less efficient, federation is inescapable if the British Caribbean territories are to cease to parade themselves to the twentieth century world as eighteenth century anachronisms. It is from this point of view, and only from this point of view that I have frequently stated that any federation is better than no federation.[10]

Thus Williams and the PNM, new on the political scene, made a fresh impact on the federal position. But it produced no spark. The general attitude was that of unemotional acceptance of the federal superstructure, accompanied in some cases by hard-eyed bargaining for unit advantages. During the two-year regime of the Standing Federation Committee (see next chapter), its members seemed to be united chiefly in their determination to clip the wings of the Federal Government that was to succeed them, and Manley's warnings in 1947 about the "vested interest of ambition in power" and willingness to "give up local roots of power for the creation of a larger centre of power" appeared in 1958 (to those who remembered them) in the light of predictions.

The timing of island elections in relation to the federal election had a significant bearing on the course of events. It was fortunate that the general elections in Jamaica in 1955 and in Trinidad in 1956 brought into power parties affiliated or associated with the West Indian Federal Labor Party, which embraced the parties in power in all except two of the other islands. On the other hand, the fact that only at these elections were the leaders of these two governments coming into office for the first time, had the unfortunate result that neither Manley nor Williams felt

10. Eric Williams, lecture delivered at Woodford Square, Jan. 5, 1956, in *Federation, Two Public Lectures* (Trinidad, 1956), pp. 11–12.

able to leave their freshly assumed island responsibilities to take part in the Federal Government. So that tensions and strains inevitably developed between these two largest and economically best-off islands and the newly established and financially weak and dependent federation which would almost certainly have been avoided if the governments in power in these two islands had been strongly represented in the Federal Parliament and Council of State.

CHAPTER 2

THE BREAK-UP OF THE FEDERATION

I.

The Federation had a slow and painful start, and the course of events which led eventually (though not inevitably) to its disintegration began soon after it had been legally instituted. The agreement to federate was signed on February 23, 1956, but two years were to elapse before the Federal Government came into existence. In the interval a Standing Federation Committee, representative of the federating governments,[1] performed the functions of a constitutional convention and a provisional government. Though acting in the name and on behalf of the West Indies, they, like the conferences before them, gave the impression of being intent on promoting or preserving insular rather than general interests. In particular they erred on the ungenerous side when they deprived the Federal Government of the little financial leeway the 1956 Conference had left to it.

The constitution came into operation with the arrival of the Governor General, Lord Hailes, who took office at Port-of-Spain on January 3, 1958, and immediately called for elections to the House of Representatives. At this stage the Federation suffered its first public setback. Norman Manley, Premier of Jamaica, the largest island, and recently elected Leader of the West Indies Federal Labor Party, which the dominant parties in nearly all the islands either belonged to or were expected to support, de-

1. The three most important in terms of population were Jamaica, Trinidad, and Barbados. The Units in the Windward group were Grenada, St. Vincent, St. Lucia, and Dominica, and those in the Leeward group were Antigua, St. Kitts-Nevis-Anguilla, and Montserrat. (The Cayman, Turks, and Caicos Islands are dependencies of Jamaica, and Tobago is combined with Trinidad in a political entity.) For area and population of the federating Units see Appendix B. See also the map opposite page 1.

clined to stand for election to the Federal Parliament. This decision probably had a discouraging effect on the growth of federal sentiment in Jamaica. It undoubtedly contributed to his party's disastrous defeat in the federal elections; in spite of its being the party in power in the island government, its candidates secured only five seats out of a total of seventeen.

Sir Grantley Adams, Premier of Barbados and one of the veteran leaders of the labor movement in the Caribbean, who had been President of the CLC at the height of its influence in September 1947 and was now the first Deputy Leader of the Federal Labor Party, was pressed into service and became the first Prime Minister of the West Indies. He took office with the slimmest of majorities, and it took all his considerable political and parliamentary skill to keep his government from defeat during the first anxious session.

It was during this first session that the Federal Parliament took the decision that led to the beginning of a review of the federal constitution within the second year of its life. Article 118 of the constitution provided that not later than the fifth anniversary of the date on which the constitution came into force there should be convened a conference of delegates from the Federation itself, from each of the Units and from the United Kingdom for the purpose of reviewing the constitution. The article required that this conference should "among other things, review, in the light of the progress made towards establishing a customs union within the Federation and other relevant factors, the powers conferred by this Constitution on the Federal Legislature to make provision for the levying of taxes on income and profits."

In June 1958, Mr. Ken Hill of Jamaica, a member of the Opposition, moved for the appointment of a Select Committee of the House to take such steps as were necessary to achieve the goal of self-government and Dominion Status within the Commonwealth at the earliest possible moment. The Government proposed an amendment, which was carried, calling for the convening, not later than June 1959, of the conference envisaged by article 118 of the constitution, "in order to achieve the goal of self government and Dominion Status within the Commonwealth at the earliest possible date." The Government later decided to

[13]

summon the Unit Governments to a preliminary conference to discuss various points of view and to work out a pattern of proposals that could be put to Her Majesty's Government at the conference provided for by the constitution. This preliminary conference eventually met on September 28, 1959.

The demand for a review of the constitution within the very first session of the Federal Parliament came as a surprise to most West Indians. The proposal was prompted, in large measure at any rate, by dissatisfaction with the "colonial" limitations contained in the federal constitution. In particular, objection was taken to the powers reserved to the Queen in Council. These pertained to foreign affairs, and to securing the financial stability and preserving the credit of the Federation (and thus safeguarding the financial liability of the United Kingdom Government). The discretionary powers of the Governor General, particularly in the appointment of Senators, and his position as President of the Council of State, were also objected to, as was the presence of three officials on the Council. These were transitional provisions, it is true, but at a time when full internal self-government had been or was about to be granted to the Unit governments, there was wide support for the view that the period of transition should be short.

So far as the Queen's reserve powers were concerned, the Federal Government was in a somewhat false position in relation to those Unit Governments that had achieved internal self-government. In the colonial context, the absence of such reserve powers in Unit constitutions was possible only because the matters they affected had been transferred to the new government at the center. The logic of the situation therefore required that the Federal Government move on to independence as soon as possible.

This logic appealed strongly to Dr. Eric Williams, the Premier of Trinidad; and he and his party, the People's National Movement, assumed the leadership of those who were demanding an early advance to dominion status. In the meantime, however, Jamaica had been having afterthoughts about her position in the Federation and had become more concerned with the objective of reducing the powers of the Federal Government in relation to Jamaica than with that of putting an end to its colonial status.

[14]

II.

The eve of the Intergovernmental Conference therefore found these two major islands poles apart. Trinidad wished the Federation to assume dominion status almost immediately and proposed a firm date—April 22, 1960. The constitution must therefore be amended to give it full control of its own affairs, free from outside interference or intervention from any source. The PNM publicly declared that the federal constitution should be based on a clear-cut and comprehensive conception aimed at securing the following major objectives: (1) national independence and security; (2) the development of a national spirit; (3) the basic human freedoms, including freedom of religious worship; and (4) the economic development and integration of the area. The PNM would strengthen the Federal Government and increase its powers as against the powers of the Units, giving it, in particular, powers of taxation in all fields (the portions of revenue to be refunded to the Units being arranged by agreement with the Unit Governments). The Federal Government would also have the final word in legislation on other matters affecting planning and development of all kinds, including banking and the raising of external loans.

The PNM proposals, which had been approved by a party conference at the beginning of September, were published by the Government in a booklet entitled *The Economics of Nationhood*. They were approved by the Legislative Council in a debate that concluded with the passing of a resolution endorsing the principle of a strong, independent Federation vested with appropriate powers and responsibilities, and giving a mandate to the Trinidad and Tobago delegation to the Intergovernmental Conference to seek the support of the other Units for such amendments to the federal constitution as would be necessary to achieve this goal and enable the West Indies Federation to take its proper place in the Commonwealth and in the United Nations.

The Economics of Nationhood assumed that the common purpose was to build a West Indian nation and argued that since the first objective of the nation must be to build a national economy, the national government must be enabled to do this by being given "complete command of all its material and other resources, including its perspective for the future" (p. 3). The section dealing with the financial relationship between the Federal and the Unit Governments concludes with the following (p. 11):

> Only a powerful and centrally directed economic co-ordination and interdependence can create the true foundations of a nation. Barbados will not unify with British Guiana, or Jamaica with Antigua. They will be knit together only through their common allegiance to a Central Government. Anything else will discredit the conception of a Federation and in the end leave the islands more divided than before.

Jamaica took the opposite stand and insisted that the power of the Federal Government to intervene in Jamaican affairs should be severely limited. Even the existing constitution, in her view, gave the Federal Government too large a power to interfere with the industrial development of each unit and with its powers of taxation. She demanded[2] that the constitution be revised so as to exclude the possibility of federal control, and to leave in the control of each unit the development of industry and the power to levy income tax, excise duties and consumption taxes. For the sake of those of the smaller islands that might desire to establish a closer relation with the Federal Government, Jamaica proposed that a constitutional formula be devised which would enable such Units to entrust the Federal Government with a greater range of powers over their internal affairs, yet still leave a Unit like Jamaica free to have a looser association with the federal center and keep control over all matters which, in her view, she could take care of for herself.

In this connection Jamaica laid great emphasis on the importance of machinery for consultation between the Federation and the Units at the highest level. She proposed that some such body as the Regional Council of Ministers be officially recognized as the body which would discuss such policy differences as might arise on matters of common concern and all proposals for transfer to the center of functions previously performed by a Unit.

The Jamaican proposals included also the demand that

2. Ministry Paper No. 18, May 27, 1959.

representation in the elected house of the Federal Legislature be on the basis of population—a demand which, though justifiable on grounds of precedent and theory, came as a surprise to the other Units. They had grown used to a formula for the distribution of seats which was based on a combination of other factors with that of population, and which had remained virtually unaltered during some ten years of constitution-making. Jamaica also insisted that the steps toward customs union be not hurried; and on the question of dominion status, in contrast to Trinidad's demand for independence on April 22, 1960, Jamaica was content to say that the Federal Government should seek it "as soon as was practicable and possible."

The Jamaican demands, like the Trinidadian proposals, were debated in the Legislature; and the Jamaican delegation, which included representatives of the Opposition, came to the conference with a unanimous mandate.

Jamaica and Trinidad thus were diametrically opposed in their conception of the role to be played by the Federal Government and the powers it should have. Fears were expressed that the adoption by the major Units of the Federation of positions on the face of them irreconcilable might result in the early break-up of the Federation. Those who regarded themselves as West Indians found little to question in the Trinidad proposals, except perhaps the date for independence. The issue as they saw it was well stated by Dr. Elsa Goveia:

It is important to ask what this nation is. If it includes all the people of the Federation, the national Government is the government of the Federation. That Government must be given powers commensurate with its responsibilities. Otherwise it will prove to be as impotent in the face of the needs and desires of its citizens as was Crown Colony government in relation to its subjects. Changes of government will be meaningless until we have settled the fundamental question of our national identity. In the earlier struggle for our political rights, it was perhaps enough to be anti-British. Now that we face Independence, and the immense problems which it will bring, it has become ab-

[17]

solutely essential that we should know whether we are West
Indians.[3]

Trinidad's demand for a strong federation without delay
raised no new issues of principle, only of ways and means. The
Jamaican proposals on the other hand, would change the character of the Federation.

III.

This may be a good place to pause and inquire how Jamaica's
change of attitude came about. A number of causes contributed
to it. The chief one was the improvement in Jamaica's economic
position since 1947. While agricultural production and income
increased and tourism expanded, mining and secondary industries
also entered the picture. Bauxite production began in 1952 and
rose from one million tons in 1953 to nearly six million in 1958.
Moreover, the Government, by renegotiating in 1957 the terms
of its agreement with the bauxite companies, greatly increased
Jamaica's immediate and prospective income from this source.
Tourism had been expanding continuously since the war and by
1958 was contributing nearly as much to the national income as
sugar. In the promotion of secondary industries, which she had
embarked on at the beginning of the decade, Jamaica was achieving an encouraging measure of success.

Whereas, therefore, in 1947 her economic position had been
such that it was natural to believe that union with the eastern
Caribbean territories, including oil-rich Trinidad, was the best
if not the only avenue to economic improvement, by 1958 the
position had changed:[4] it was possible to hope with some con-

3. *An Introduction to the Federation Day Exhibition* (University College
of the West Indies, 1959), p. 40.

4. The following figures reveal the degree of diversification that had taken
place.

Jamaica Gross Domestic Product Percentages

	1938	1950	1956	1959
Agriculture	36.2	30.8	16.4	13.4
Mining	—	—	5.5	8.4
Manfacturing	6.5	11.3	13.2	12.9
Construction and installation	3.5	7.6	12.7	11.4
	[46.2]	[49.7]	[47.8]	[46.1]

Sources: *The National Income of Jamaica*, 1956, Table 3A, p. 48, and *Economic Survey, Jamaica*, 1959, p. 7.

[18]

fidence that Jamaica would achieve on her own the self-sustaining economic growth that would lead her eventually into the ranks of the "modernized" and "developed" countries.

In this situation it was easy for tension to arise between the West Indies Federal Government and the Government of Jamaica. The federal capital was a thousand miles away in Port-of-Spain. The Prime Minister was not a Jamaican. This fact alone was hard for Jamaicans to bear. They still had little contact with the eastern islands and assumed a superiority corresponding to their size; West Indian sentiment in Jamaica was a young and tender plant, at an early stage of growth and not well nourished. The poor showing of the People's National Party (PNP) in the federal elections had had the result that the representatives of Jamaica in the federal cabinet were not persons of eminence. Powerful influences in or near the Jamaican cabinet were still unconvinced that the Federation was a good thing for Jamaica and were actively hostile to it. (Opposition from these quarters diminished, if it did not entirely disappear, as the intergovernmental discussions proceeded between 1959 and 1961 and seemed increasingly likely to result in decisions favorable to Jamaica.)

The relation between the role of Sir Grantley Adams as Federal Prime Minister and that of Mr. Norman Manley as Leader of the Federal Labor Party (and at the same time Premier of Jamaica) was not in the circumstances an easy one for either of the two men to sustain. Even a Prime Minister who had not just experienced a decade of political supremacy in Barbados, as Sir Grantley had done, might have been irked by the position of financial stringency and helplessness in which the Federal Government found itself. Sir Grantley's reaction was to hint publicly that the Federal Government, as soon as it had the power to impose taxation on income and profits, might decide to exercise it with retroactive effect. The fact that the next general elections in Jamaica were no more than a year away, and probably less, almost certainly intensified the sharpness of the public reaction that these veiled threats produced. Bustamante and his Opposition party seized on them (as they did even on so harmless and necessary a measure as the federal Compulsory Land Acquisition Law) to embarrass the Government party, and in this way were assisted by the element of surprise.

[19]

The realization that the Federal Government was a separate entity which might do things that would affect Jamaica was a shocking experience for a large number of Jamaicans. Until the Federal Parliament was actually functioning, very few Jamaicans had paid any attention to the meaning or implications of federation; and nothing was done to bring the reality of it home to them except the publication of occasional news of conferences and reports and occasional lectures organized by the University College of the West Indies and by groups of private citizens.

It was the visit of the Governor General in 1958 that first brought a sense of the Federation's reality to the common people, especially those who lived outside Kingston. Outside the small circle of those involved directly or indirectly in the making of government policy, serious thought about the implications of federation for Jamaica's political position began with the Prime Minister's references to retroactive taxation. Until then the Federation had been accepted in Jamaica as something external —the firm assumption being that nothing in Jamaica's position would be changed.

The public reaction was excited and sometimes abusive. Most said that the Prime Minister was bluffing and that his bluff should be called; some few believed he could make good his threat and were humiliated at the thought. Said one writer in Jamaica's leading newspaper, the *Gleaner,* on December 5, 1958: "I am shocked that now Jamaica can be dictated to by small islanders even under the guise of creating a large nation." There was an appeal to unity, and numerous letters appeared in the *Gleaner* harping on this note. One political commentator went so far as to castigate the Jamaican members of the Federal House of Representatives for being loyal to the Federal Government and the federal party rather than to the PNP of Jamaica.

There was also emphasis on the need for thinking afresh. The *Gleaner* echoed this sentiment on December 7 in an editorial comment to the effect that "Jamaica went into this federation without clear thought as to the design of the dwelling" (and the writer went on to put the blame on the Colonial Office). It also echoed another general sentiment which followed after the first angry reaction, namely, that the debate which had been started was salutary: "Let the people talk, but let them think carefully before they talk." This advice was necessary. Strong insular-nationalistic feelings had been aroused and these feelings were bound to be exploited by the Opposition for political purposes, especially with general elections just around the corner.

The annual conference of the Jamaica Labor Party (JLP), which met in Kingston on November 23, 1958, passed a resolution giving full and unqualified support to a motion that had been moved in the Federal Parliament by Mr. Robert Lightbourne, one of the Jamaican members of the Opposition in the Federal House of Representatives. This motion called for immediate revision of the federal constitution in order to eliminate the power of retroactive taxation and interference with tariff structures without Jamaica's consent, and to provide for representation in the House of Representatives on the basis of population. A visiting Trinidadian Member of the Federal Parliament who addressed the conference was loudly cheered when he made reference to the threat of retroactive taxation and said it was wrong to take chances with the economy of Jamaica or Trinidad. But when he went on to say that federation was needed for the creation of a new West Indian nation, he was received in cold silence; and Sir Alexander, who spoke after him, repudiated the idea that it was necessary for Jamaica to achieve nationhood through the Federation. He was obviously already beginning to move toward the stand he eventually took some eighteen months later, when he withdrew his party's candidate from a federal by-election and declared his party against Jamaica's continuing in the federal scheme.

The *Gleaner* summed up the prevailing feeling in an end of year editorial:

Federation has dominated Jamaica's horizon in this year which has come to a close and will be its dilemma in the year which starts tomorrow. The Jamaican elections which are some months away—at the most twelve—will reflect the national preoccupation about the commitment to become part of a sovereign and overriding new government of the West Indies.

If Mr. Manley and Sir Alexander Bustamante hid in a back room when candidates for federal election were chosen for the first time, other men from other islands have not,

[21]

and now bid fair to take hold of Jamaica's destiny and affairs to a degree that already seems alarming. Sir Grantley Adams has shed the chrysalis shroud of a Manley grub and fully armed with mandibles, darts like a sinister dragonfly over the West Indian pond.

It was clear that in the coming election campaign Bustamante's Oppositon party would hold up the image of Sir Grantley as an anti-Jamaican bogy man, and use his association with the PNP as a weapon against them. "If Mr. Manley is to win," said a *Gleaner* correspondent on December 29, "he had better take heed and show himself no less a good Jamaican than his rival." (Manley took this advice and won the general elections, which were held in July 1959.)

Thus by the end of 1958 the pending Intergovernmental Conference, called originally for the almost "routine" purpose of considering the steps that would lead the West Indies to dominion status as quickly as possible, came to assume from Jamaica the aspect of a battle ground, where the issues embodied in Lightbourne's motion in the Federal House of Representatives in November (later to be endorsed unanimously by both parties in the Jamaican parliament) would be fought to a finish—the issues of representation in the Federal House in accordance with population and abstention by the Federal Government from intervention in matters of economic development and income and profits taxation, at any rate in Jamaica.

Manley had an early opportunity of emphasizing the importance he attached to reserving to the Unit Governments full freedom of action for industrial development when in January 1959, at a meeting of the Regional Consultative Council (which there and then assumed the title of Regional Council of Ministers), he used this argument in successfully opposing the Prime Minister's proposal that a joint statement on economic development and investment be issued by Federal and Unit Governments.

It is easy to show by evidence selectively gathered after the event that the change in attitude toward the Federation on the part of the two Jamaican parties had occurred as early as the turn of the year 1958–59; but to those who lived through these events the indications at the time were far from clear.[5] Important statements were often buried in a welter of emotion, and the newspaper reader's attention to events was, by journalistic convention, directed wherever possible less to the important than to the dramatic. Moreover, the general election campaigns were being waged with great fervor and it was difficult to know how much of what was said by the rival parties should be discounted for this reason. Thus it was that the other units were in fact surprised by the nature of the firm and unequivocal mandate with which the Jamaican delegation came to Port-of-Spain in September 1959.

IV.

When the conference duly opened on September 28, the delegations from the other governments still had not quite recovered from the shock of the Jamaican proposals; and it soon became clear that the issues raised would not be quickly disposed of. As it turned out, some twenty months of study and discussion were needed to achieve a consensus. The first session of the conference lasted ten days and resulted in agreement in principle that population was to be the basis of representation in the elected house of the Federal Parliament. The method of application of this principle, as well as the other constitutional changes and political and economic arrangements implied in the advance to dominion status, were referred for detailed consideration to two committees of Ministers, which were to be assisted by working parties of Officials.

It was now clear to all that continuance of the federal union would depend on the possibility of the other Units coming to terms with Jamaica. Manley went home in a hopeful frame of

5. But the following comment by a Jamaican writer two and a half years later may be of interest: "While every aspect of Federation had been discussed and debated by the other units since 1948, it did not become even half real for Jamaicans despite the fact that it was conceived and born on their own doorstep, until Sir Grantley Adams spoke out of turn a couple of years ago. Since then the Federation has had plenty of publicity, but mostly bad and certainly not enlightening. The P.N.P. leaders, from Mr. Manley down, were lukewarm to hostile until the Premier came out firmly in favour after his London visit last year: while the J.L.P., desperate for a stick with which to beat their rivals, have railed against Federation without moderation or conscience." Clinton Parchment, "Federation—Jamaica's Safeguard," *Gleaner,* June 26, 1961.

mind, and on arrival at the airport announced that Jamaica would stay in the Federation, an announcement that was given headlines in the press and much criticized by the JLP opposition. A fortnight later, at the annual conference of the PNP, Manley described the party's policy on federation in the following words:

> We conceive that in the long run there are real and great advantages in Federation but those advantages cannot be accepted at the price of anything that would destroy or injure us in a fundamental respect. That is a workable policy and that is the policy I propose to fight for.[6]

This was the stand he took in the House of Representatives on November 3 when he made an important speech[7] in the debate on the Government's report on the September–October session of the Intergovernmental Conference. He restated the Jamaican position and argued at length in support of it. He emphasized that what his government was seeking was "a framework for a Dominion which could take a respectable, modest place in the world community of nations" and "satisfy the ambitions of those of our people who think nationhood is a worthwhile ambition"; but it must be conceived "not in terms of the strongest and most centralised federation you could think of" but of one that "would allow for a Unit like Jamaica the maximum freedom of development in accordance with the plan we have elaborated for our own development."

Manley took the opportunity of recalling the reasons why the parties in Jamaica had agreed "over a period of nine years, in eight full-scale debates—and on every occasion unanimously—that federation was a desirable move." First there was what he called the ambition of nationhood. "It started off in the days when people regarded the cause of national freedom as of high significance . . . when there was great faith and strong feeling in this country," and people in Jamaica, he said, more and more met people from other islands and realized that they were in fact one people of similar historical origin and racial admixture, with similar problems and a natural affinity when they met.

6. *Gleaner*, Oct. 26, 1959.
7. *Proceedings of the House of Representatives*, p. 95 ff.

People noticed how more and more West Indians were compelled to do more and more things together—cricket, Chambers of Commerce, Sugar Producers Associations, the university—"so that in the course of years there was almost no aspect of West Indies life which was not linked to some form of West Indies association. . . ."

"And then people noticed that in order that those things should go smoothly the West Indies politicians had found it necessary to meet together to have a forum for common discussion and simple planning." With this evidence, people "began to think that federalism had significant advantages." In his view, "the basic reasons that led Jamaica to agree with the rest of the West Indies in thinking that Federation was the best course to pursue were soundly conceived, and subject to certain qualifications . . . would be soundly conceived today." The world trend was toward aggregation of units, not separation, as was shown by the European Common Market, and a similar arrangement in South America. The Regional Economic Committee (REC) had been making great strides in evolving a common economic policy for the British Caribbean area, and had therefore been held up both as an example of the potency of federal activity and as a proof of the need for federation. The REC had had no power to make decisions, and therefore there had always been delay in the carrying out by a number of different legislatures of the policy agreed on by the committee. Thus, said Manley, to the ambition of nationhood was added the growing realization that there were practical economic considerations.

What then was the present position? "What has happened," he said, "is that the beginning of Federation has coincided almost with the climax of the combination of activities which have been undertaken by Jamaica with a view to a transition to a higher level of economy. And that has enormously complicated the problem of Federation," since for this reason "the Federation must proceed more slowly than other Federations have proceeded in the past. Jamaica," he said, "has the highest percentage of unemployment of any country in the West Indies[8]

8. Manley repeated this argument at the May 1961 session of the Intergovernmental Conference in Port-of-Spain, giving the figures as 18 percent over all and 38 percent among women (IGC Report, sec. 159).

[25]

... consequently there is no part of the West Indies in which any disruption of the forward progress would be more damaging and disastrous; and not alone for Jamaica . . . but also to the whole future of the Federation." He rejected the argument that the first and most fruitful task of the Federation was to develop the economies of the smaller islands. This was a fundamental task, but it would not show immediate returns on a significant scale, especially since the path of their development lay largely in agriculture; and in the meantime "anything that disturbs the pace of the development of Trinidad or Jamaica would be destructive of the ambitions of the Federation itself."

To those who asked, "Why can't Jamaica become a dominion on her own?" he answered, "I believe she could; but I know she would not have the significance in the world that the West Indies would have." He believed that "a West Indian nation would play a part in history that no one unit could hope to play by itself . . . I see it already happening: to state that you are a native of the West Indies gives you a status which you could not have two years ago." From a practical point of view, he believed "it would be better to go about as a group of independent people than to go about as independent beggars with ten caps in ten hands." On the level of services, experience had already shown the value of joint effort. "If Jamaica had a university on its own it would be a tremendous strain on our own resources. I believe that it would be better to handle our trading resources together. . . . I believe it will be possible to work out an economy and trade policy which will be good for the area as a whole. I do not believe that it is right to say that any form of customs union would injure Jamaica. . . . I know of many industrialists who have turned their eyes towards the West Indies because of federation."

The question, therefore, as he saw it, was whether an acceptable federal structure could be found to secure the building up of the area as a whole and at the same time not interfere with Jamaica's development program. He hoped they could work out an acceptable plan. He believed it was possible to find a solution to the problem and that it was worth while to try. If it did not prove to be possible, then he would not regard federation as the practical expedient for the advancement of the people.

I have reported Manley's statement of Jamaica's position at some length because it has assumed added importance in the light of subsequent events. I shall have to refer to it again in connection with two other parts of the story. The first concerns the Federal Government; the second will be about the referendum.

V.

Manley criticized the Federal Government on the grounds that it had failed to get to grips with the real problems, had done little to create in the West Indies an understanding of the common problems of the area, and, instead of building up a sense of confidence and hope about the future, had established a sense of fear and frustration. These criticisms no doubt found a receptive audience on the occasion when they were spoken. But to other audiences they would have lost something of their edge by the inevitable reflection that the unduly dependent position of the Federal Government, especially with regard to its finances, was calculated to produce a degree of frustration, humiliation, and loss of morale. The *Nation*, official organ of the PNM of Trinidad, in an editorial on September 16, 1959, had this to say in their defense:

> Criticisms of the Government have been many. They are too often made without a sense of proportion, springing from ignorance of politics in general and the special conditions in which the Federal Government operates. The Constitution by which it must guide itself is an abortion. Its budget is a mockery. It lacks the stimulus which can come only from complete responsibility. Elsewhere in this issue a writer deals with the profound consequences for any political regime which exists in a state of semi-independence and semi-colonialism. All suffer and none more than the regime itself. The way out of this is to change the Constitution, not the Government.

Nevertheless one could wish that the Federal Government had found it possible to show its recognition of the importance of economic development and the integration of the West Indian economies in what was perhaps the only way open to it, in view of its financial limitations, namely, by the appointment of a

[27]

strong economic advisory and planning staff under leadership of international repute. Such a staff could have won the respect of the young and enthusiastic planning staffs of Jamaica and Trinidad, and secured from them a measure of cooperation, and perhaps even of recognition of moral leadership, which would not have been without effect on the political side of their governments.

As it was, the Government, faced with a difficult choice, gave priority to other matters; with the result that on this question of economic development, which was the chief preoccupation of the major Unit Governments, the Federal Government failed to win respect or confidence. On the contrary, Jamaica, on the one hand, regarded as confirmed her instinctive apprehension that her plans for economic development would be jeopardized if the Federal Government were allowed to intervene in them, while the Government of Trinidad, intellectually convinced as they were that economic planning for the West Indies could be effective only if controlled by a strong federal government at the center, felt disappointment and impatience at the Federal Government's failure to give a lead.

VI.

While the intergovernmental committees and working parties were doing their work behind the scenes the Jamaica Government did two things, the causes of which are open to various interpretations, and which may possibly have been interconnected. Whatever their causes or connections, they proved to be important for the future of the Federation.

First, in January 1960, Manley led a delegation to London to inquire of the Colonial Secretary what were the minimum requirements for dominion status, and whether Jamaica could hope to achieve this status on her own. The answer to the latter question was in the affirmative, and this considerably strengthened Jamaica's bargaining position in forthcoming discussions with the other West Indian governments. It is a sign of the times that no one expected Britain to intervene to save the Federation,[9] though some secretly hoped she would. In a

9. Since the referendum result and the decision to dissolve the Federation, criticisms of Britain and in particular of Colonial Secretary Macleod have appeared in the press both in Britain and in the West Indies.

different age, Britain's influence played an important part in leading New Brunswick and British Columbia into the Canadian Federation and in preventing Western Australia from seceding from the federal Commonwealth of Australia. But in our time, the Government of the United Kingdom has evidently not regarded it as a British interest that West Indian unity should be preserved. Her attention has been deeply engaged with more pressing problems in other places—in Africa, in Europe, in Britain itself—and perhaps we should not forget that the Monroe Doctrine was invented in Britain.

The other thing Manley and his Government did in this connection is more difficult to explain. At the end of May 1960, they decided that the issue of Jamaica's remaining in the Federation or not was to be submitted to a referendum of the people. This decision followed immediately upon the action of Sir Alexander Bustamante and the JLP in withdrawing their candidate from the federal by-election and declaring that from then on they were opposed to federation. The reason given by Premier Manley in his official statement is as follows:

> The official decision of the Jamaica Labour Party to oppose Federation has created a new situation in Jamaica. When both parties were acting together it was right to assume that they represented the voice of the people. Now that one Party, the Jamaica Labour Party, has officially resolved to oppose Federation it is right that it should come before the people for decision.[10]

This was a *volte face* from the position adopted by Manley a few months before. The question of a referendum had been mooted shortly after the first session of the Intergovernmental Conference and in the peroration of his speech on November 3, 1959, Manley had dismissed the suggestion firmly and unequivocally. He had said:

> There are men who say today 'go to the people—take a referendum.' Maybe it will come to that, but not now. It would be a betrayal of responsibility to do that. Let me

10. *Gleaner*, June 1, 1960.

repeat. It would be a betrayal of leadership and a betrayal of responsibility to do that now.

The people did not put us here to go back to ask them what to do. The people put us here on a stated policy to fight to achieve certain ends. When we fail to achieve those ends, that is the time we are to go back to the people and say, 'Look, it cannot be done, do you think we should turn back?' That is the time. To that I pledge myself and I pledge my Government. . . .

To go and ask the people whether it is good for Jamaica to stay in Federation? Mr. Speaker, have we lost all sense of responsibility to the people? When we are ready to go and tell the people that for this or that or the other reason, 'get out,' we will tell them so, but until you have decided that the time has come when it is our duty to say so then we will tell them that we are going to continue to fight and ask them to trust us as they have trusted us in the past and ask them to trust us in the future and tell them why they should.[11]

This view would, I think, be accepted by the majority of West Indians who have given thought to constitutional questions. They would argue that the democratic way to decide a complex matter is through discussion and consensus by competent and adequately informed representatives, and that therefore to decide on such a matter by referendum is essentially undemocratic.[12]

11. *Proceedings of the House of Representatives,* p. 102.

12. An interesting commentary is provided by the resolution passed by the PNM of Trinidad on January 27, 1962, which contains the party's decision to reject unequivocally any participation in the proposed Federation of the Eastern Caribbean and "proceed forthwith to National Independence." The resolution is in four parts and the fourth part reads as follows:
AND BE IT FURTHER RESOLVED, that P.N.M.'s Government of Trinidad and Tobago take steps to consult responsible organisations in the Territory, political, economic, social, civic, cultural and fraternal, with respect to the above Resolution, in order to implement the Government's pledge contained in His Excellency the Governour's speech from the Throne on December 29, 1961, to associate the people of the Territory actively with the discussions on independence in the context of P.N.M.'s objective for achievement of an educated democracy.

VII.

The Intergovernmental Conference resumed in Port-of-Spain on May 2, 1961, and during the fortnight that followed the issues on which Jamaica had taken a firm stand were settled in a manner acceptable to her—all but one. This was a corollary to the decision that there should be a Reserve List of legislative powers that would include the development of industries and taxes on income and profits. There was an inconclusive debate on the question of the procedure for amending the Constitution to transfer items from the Reserve List. Most of the delegates objected to the method proposed by Jamaica on the ground that it gave Jamaica a permanent veto. But Premier Manley said he had pledged himself to it by announcement to his Parliament in March 1960, after he had received the British Government's assurances that Jamaica would not be subjected to undue pressure or to force if she were to leave the Federation, and after he had had discussions with the Premier of Trinidad and Tobago with respect to the Reserve List and to a procedure that would fully protect and safeguard the Jamaican position.

In the debate on this question the Premier of Trinidad and Tobago, Dr. Williams, made an important statement recorded in the official conference report as follows:

292. . . . In order to assess the merits of the Jamaica case in respect of the Reserve List, Trinidad and Tobago had made a serious analysis of Jamaica's economic position. They had become aware of the tremendous unemployment problem that Jamaica faces. They were aware that migration to the United Kingdom between 1955 and 1960 amounted to well over 100,000 persons. What was more disturbing was that despite the tremendous development of Puerto Rico's economy within recent years, the Puerto Ricans had not been able to make any real dent in the unemployment problem. A larger proportion of the population was dependent upon agriculture in Jamaica than was the case in Trinidad, and the average income in agriculture was just a little more than one-third of the average income in industry. Further, the proportion was much smaller than the proportion in Jamaica. He understood fully the difficulties

[31]

of the Jamaica situation in respect of industrial development, high cost production, extensive use of quantitative restrictions, and taking the maximum advantage of their non-association with the General Agreement on Tariffs and Trade. He could understand the concern of the Jamaica Government in respect of Jamaica's distressing dependence on exports of a commodity like bauxite where the problem of stockpiling by a foreign power was involved. He could understand Jamaica's concern about the inherent instability of foreign earnings derived from the tourist trade. The problems inherent in a new pattern of world trade (common to all Territories) were of supreme concern to the Jamaica Government—whether it was a question of Commonwealth preferences, whether it involved citrus from the United States, cigars from Cuba, the problem of dollar liberalisation in the United Kingdom or the problem of competition in the banana industry from the Cameroons and other African territories or the recent problems of the sugar industry. And above all the specific problems there was the supreme problem of the European Common Market. As regards income tax, the Jamaican Government had gone further than any West Indian Government in utilising income tax, and exemptions from income tax, as incentives to production, especially to export production.

293. Jamaica had put its case before the Conference. It was not enough to say that one did not agree with Jamaica. It was essential to try to understand her position. Approximately 40% of the Federal revenue is to come from Jamaica. Trinidad and Tobago alone could not take over the responsibilities involved in a Federation without Jamaica. This was especially so in view of the rejection of the Trinidad and Tobago plan for Federation as a result of which the contribution of Trinidad and Tobago was to be substantially increased without any corresponding transfer of services to the Federal Government. In his view Jamaica had conspicuously underestimated the advantages it would derive from Federation. In recent weeks Jamaicans had been emphasising the economies which Jamaica would stand to make in matters of defence and international relations. They

appear to overlook that with all the grave difficulties facing The West Indies with respect to impending international negotiations, the international personality of a West Indian Federation would be infinitely superior to that which any individual Territory could muster. As regards the customs union plan, Jamaica feared competition from the industry of Trinidad and Tobago. It was well that this relatively gentle competition was available to prepare them when they come to deal with the hostile world outside The West Indies.

294. He did not agree with the Jamaican fears with respect to Federal control of industry. Trinidad and Tobago had similar problems to those of Jamaica but was yet prepared to submit to Federal control. Jamaica was falling into the common mistake of considering a particular Government instead of a Federation which the Territories were all trying to create. Nevertheless, Trinidad and Tobago could understand and sympathise with the Jamaican case and had tried to meet them most of the way.

Dr. Williams expressed disappointment at the Jamaican insistence on the particular formula they were proposing, which went beyond the principle of representation by population and gave Jamaica a permanent veto. The conference eventually agreed to Mr. Manley's suggestion that the matter be allowed to stand out of the agenda, so that on his return to Jamaica he would be able to discover whether or not there was an alternative acceptable to those concerned.

No such alternative proposal had been found when the Constitutional Conference (provided for under Article 118 of the constitution) duly met in London on May 31. The report of the conference, signed only by the Secretary of State and by an Official who had acted as Secretary General, explained that:

44. With so many delegations present at the Conference it was inevitable that certain delegations should find themselves not in agreement with some of the conclusions set out in Chapter III of this Report. Many indeed recorded dissent on particular items. It was recognised that the conclusions reached at Lancaster House were ad referendum

[33]

to Legislatures. The Secretary of State made it clear that, in accepting the scheme as a whole for the purpose of presentation to their legislatures, delegates would be fully entitled to explain the stand which they had taken on particular matters during the Conference.

In the main, however, it would be true to say that the threat of secession had enabled Jamaica to win agreement, sometimes reluctant, from the other Units to all the conditions which her legislature had unanimously considered to provide an adequate basis for her continued membership of the Federation. But the ultimate decision was now beyond the reach of cabinet and parliament.

The referendum on September 19, 1961, resulted in a vote of 46 percent in favor to 54 percent against Jamaica's continued membership of the Federation. The question whether Trinidad would join in a federation with the other islands of the eastern Caribbean was not answered until January 1962. In that interval the PNM won a resounding victory in the general elections in December 1961. Trinidad's decision against federation was made on January 27 by resolution at a special convention of the PNM. It is a remarkable resolution in many ways, not least for the number of recitals by which it is preceded. These recitals, twenty-four in number, give the reasons for the decisions embodied in the resolution, and it is interesting to note that the third one reads as follows:

AND WHEREAS the United Kingdom Government, at the Lancaster House Conference in London in June 1960, conceded to Jamaica a permanent veto in respect of the future assumption by the Federal Government of power to direct and promote the industrialisation of West Indian economy, but was prepared to conciliate the smaller Territories by not conceding to Trinidad and Tobago a similar veto in respect of the free movement of persons within the Federation. . . .

It was clear that Dr. Williams and the PNM took it hard that, on the one issue on which they demanded a concession, they had not in their turn received the understanding and sympathy they had shown when, against their firm convictions, they had supported the concessions to Jamaica, which they regarded as standing on no stronger grounds.

CHAPTER 3

THE CLASH OF NATIONALISMS IN
THE WEST INDIES

I.

Behind the actions and events which together make up the history of the rise and fall of the first West Indian Federation, it is possible to discern a struggle between competing nationalisms—between West Indian nationalism and island nationalisms, in particular Jamaican and, more recently, Trinidadian. By nationalism in this context is meant the assertion of selfhood by a group, in a defined geographical area, having a sentiment of belonging together, an accepted leadership, and an intention to be governed as a separate community from within and not from without—the kind of group self-assertion that in favorable circumstances can result in the creation of a nation-state.

The existence of a degree of such nationalism on the part of the units is, of course, implicit in the federal conception. The essential feature of federal government is the distribution of state power between the central government and the unit governments; so that there must exist an equilibrium between the forces of attraction exerted by the center and by the units in their several directions. Nationalism provides the force in each case. The actual process, however, of bringing a federal system into being out of previously separate units is one in which timing plays an important part; and therefore skill and care and good fortune are necessary, if the balance of uniting and separating forces is to be maintained for long enough to enable the federal institutions to be firmly established.

The trouble in the West Indies has been that the timing has not been happy and the necessary balance has not been successfully maintained. Jamaican nationalism, which found

[36]

organized expression in Jamaica at about the time that West Indian nationalism became a force in the eastern Caribbean, was for a time eclipsed by West Indian nationalism. But it survived and reasserted itself strongly enough to seize the opportunity, fortuitously given to it in the referendum, of defeating its rival, as it were, on the tape. Trinidadian nationalism, on the other hand, was late in developing and came to maturity just in time to beckon Trinidad and Tobago to follow in the footsteps of Jamaica to independence as a separate state.

II.

The disturbances, strikes, and riots of the 1930's were more than acts of self-assertion by the people actually taking part. These gestures of revolt released the pent-up dissatisfaction with existing political and social conditions on the part of all classes in the several communities—all except the most privileged, whose members had nothing to gain from political and social change. The disturbances set off a great burst of political energy, which was immediately channelled into new or already existing political parties and trade unions and became the labor movement in the West Indies. Through these parties and unions the movement proceeded without delay to assault the political and economic power of the planter-merchant oligarchy that was entrenched in all the territories, and within less than ten years labor governments were almost everywhere in power. The British Government, having already sensed the direction of "the winds of change," gave its ready cooperation, where this was required, in bringing about the necessary political reforms. These were to lead by stages through adult suffrage and a measure of ministerial responsibility to the goal of complete responsible self-government. On the economic side, during the same period, trade-union representation and collective bargaining came to be recognized as a permanent part of the commercial and industrial life of the communities.

But the labor movement had another dimension. It was more than the instrument for remedying the social and political grievances of individuals and classes against others within their own communities. It came almost immediately to be the vehicle of the nationalist spirit (insular in Jamaica, West Indian else-

[37]

where) that had for some years now been looking for a bodily form. The distinctness of these two elements in the labor movement—the nationalist element and the element of political and social reform—can be seen most clearly in Jamaica, where the movement from the start was divided into two separate factions (and ·has maintained this division ever since) under the rival leaders Alexander Bustamante and Norman Manley. The Bustamante section of the movement had its origin in a number of small, separate unions, under enthusiastic but weak leadership. These were swept into unity as a trade union (and later on as a labor party) under the influence, and indeed under the name, of their dynamic leader. Self-conscious nationalism was not a characteristic of Bustamante's section of the movement. The Jamaica Labor Party was announced on the eve of the 1944 general election, and sailed to victory on the slogan "Vote Labor."

Manley, on the other hand, found himself in 1938 the elected leader of a group that was dominated by politically sophisticated intellectuals who were definitely nationalist and anti-imperialist in spirit; and the organization they launched to attract popular support was significantly named the People's National Party. The practice arose early, among the more reverent members, of referring to their leader as the "Father of the Nation," and the party campaigned with a national song, "Jamaica Arise." Although they lost the first two elections under the new constitution (in 1944 and 1949) to their rivals, the Jamaica Labor Party, they met no opposition from that party to their preaching of Jamaican nationalism. On the contrary, the JLP absorbed the doctrine, and it was under the banner of Jamaican nationalism that ten or fifteen years later they defeated the PNP in the referendum campaign that took Jamaica out of the West Indian Federation.

III.

In the eastern Caribbean also the labor movement became the vehicle for a nationalist spirit, with the important difference that in this case the nationalism was West Indian. A less important difference was that the nationalist spirit as it appeared in the eastern group[1] was not at any time especially identifiable with any particular organization. It came to be associated chiefly with the name of Albert Marryshow, the Grenadian legislator who founded and edited the newspaper which he deliberately named *The West Indian,* and who was greatly encouraged whenever he detected signs of the West Indian people thinking nationally.

This nationalist spirit began to show itself in the 1920's soon after the return of the West Indian troops from World War I. It had its origin in the reactions of West Indians abroad, whether as students, soldiers, or emigrants, to their common experiences as an unprivileged minority—both the need they felt for having and belonging to some nation of their own and also their recognition of the family likeness they saw in West Indians from islands other than their own. When they returned to the eastern Caribbean, where there was some degree of regular intercourse between the territories, the family feeling they had acquired persisted and grew, and the nationalist sentiments they expressed found a sympathetic response; so that by the 1930's, in this part of the region, the idea that the nation was the West Indies had come to be so completely accepted as to be taken for granted by the political leaders and others who gave thought to political questions.

IV.

West Indian nationalism was taken for granted in another sense also—in the sense that it was merely assumed, and rarely felt or pursued with passion. The West Indian leaders had come to the settled conviction that the interests of the West Indies could be adequately looked after only if West Indians made their own decisions at home and had a voice at the council tables abroad where decisions affecting their interests were made. But the West Indian movement never took on the quality of a crusade. The Homeric epithet that usually goes with nationalism is "rabid." No one has ever thought of applying this epithet in the West Indian case. The reasons are not far to seek. Rabid nationalism

1. The Leeward Islands, the Windward Islands, Barbados, Trinidad and Tobago, and for a time also British Guiana.

[39]

arises in response to long felt and long resented oppression by an alien power, or in situations where there is legal discrimination based on racial or cultural differences and where the persistent occurrence of affronts to personal dignity from motives of racial prejudice has engendered strong feelings of corporate resentment against the dominant power. This is not the situation in the West Indies where, during the century and a quarter since the abolition of slavery, equality before the law has been effectively provided for all, and where such expressions of prejudice as do occur are attributed not to external but to local origins.

Nor does there exist the motive of defending or promoting an indigenous culture in face of the encroachment of an alien one. There is in fact no indigenous culture. The West Indian communities contain a number of cultural elements, none of them indigenous; the only culture that is shared by all is the culture of the metropolitan country. Far from being alien, the metropolitan culture was there first,[2] and was the only culture recognized and fostered during the two centuries before 1838.

There was not even the excuse for a Boston Tea Party. That lesson had been learnt in Britain once for all. The West Indian grievances in the 1930's, on the political side, arose from the narrowness of the electoral franchise and the absence of responsible government and, on the economic side, were associated with a lack of the development that would provide employment and raise levels of living. Neither of these sets of grievances was of the kind to engender passionate feelings against Britain. Inevitably the Colonial Office was included among the targets for attack by the agitators for constitutional reform, since the British government was the ultimate source of power, and it was of course the one target that was common to them all. If the Colonial Office had shown intransigence in the face of local demands, strong and passionate feelings would certainly have been aroused against it. But it did not. On the contrary, the Crown was traditionally regarded as the protector of the weak, especially since the days of Queen Victoria, and the Colonial

2. The original inhabitants of the islands were Caribs or, in the case of Jamaica and Barbados, Arawaks. No Arawaks survive, and only a handful of Caribs in a remote village in Dominica. Only traces of their cultures survive, in museums.

Office had come to be generally regarded as more liberal in its attitude to the welfare and dignity of the common people than those in power locally. Strong feelings were therefore reserved for the immediate targets for attack—the local governments and legislatures, and the interest groups they represented. In any case Britain soon appeared in the role of counsellor and friend, or perhaps "uncle" is the appropriate word.

The disturbances led to the appointment of a Royal Commission whose recommendations, published in 1940, were promptly followed by the setting up of the Development and Welfare Organization (with its expert advisers, its fund for development, and its active encouragment of development planning by all the West Indian governments), and immediately afterwards by the planning and establishment, jointly by the British and West Indian Governments, of the University College of the West Indies, with the deliberate intention of assisting the West Indies in "successfully embracing the greater political independence of self-government." Finally the Secretary of State for the Colonies invited the Governments to meet him at Montego Bay in 1947 and offered them independence for the West Indies as soon as they could work out a constitutional basis for a Federal Government.

In this rarefied atmosphere of benevolent cooperation the flame of West Indian nationalism was bound to flicker and burn low. September 1947 saw the high point of West Indian nationalist feeling. The Secretary of State's conference at Montego Bay had been immediately preceded by a conference in Kingston of the Caribbean Labor Congress, which included the principal leaders of the labor movement from all the British Caribbean territories (Jamaica being represented by the Manley and not by the Bustamante section). This conference had passed what proved to be its last resolution demanding federation and independence, and had drafted its last federal constitution. The Montego Bay Conference recommended the appointment of a committee of representatives of the West Indian Governments to work out proposals which might form the basis of a federal government that would lead to West Indian independence, and this recommendation was immediately implemented by the appointment of the Rance Committee.

There was no cause left to keep West Indian nationalism fresh, and it quietly withered.

V.

The West Indian political leaders, instead of being united in demanding independence from Britain, now found themselves engaged in long drawn out negotiations with one another about the terms of a federal constitution and the structure of political and economic institutions for the proposed federal system. Negotiations of this kind, which involve bargaining and the safeguarding of selfish interests, are divisive rather than unifying, and by January 1958, when the federal constitution came into effect, the West Indian spirit was at a very low ebb. Only momentum carried forward the unifying process.

This is not to say that the break-up of the Federation was inevitable. If the process had not been tampered with, association and habit would in time have produced a sentiment of belonging together more durable than nationalist passion or intellectual conviction could produce. But time was needed. The system would have had to be preserved for long enough to achieve this result; and meanwhile, care and skill and good luck were required to get over this first, most difficult phase of unwonted intimacy.

After all, each island was, potentially, a separate little member of the British Commonwealth of Nations—overwhelmingly, or at least predominantly, British in education and culture, more accustomed to dealing with Britain than with the other islands, not conscious of being oppressed by any British yoke, but on the contrary dependent for prosperity and indeed survival upon special arrangements with Britain for the marketing of crops too small in quantity, even in the aggregate, to give much bargaining power in world markets. There was comparatively little trade between the islands and there had been virtually no communication between Jamaica and the rest until the advent of air travel, which coincided with World War II. Thus the ties between the islands themselves were weaker than the ties of each with Britain. What chiefly brought them together was the belief that because of their size they could not achieve individually the degree of political independence that would enable them to play a direct part in protecting and promoting their interests and making the best bargains in commonwealth and other international affairs.

At the time of the Montego Bay Conference this belief in the advantages of association, though recently acquired in Jamaica, was nevertheless universal. But in the eleven years that elapsed before the Federal Government came into existence, the position changed for Jamaica and Trinidad. As already related, the new bauxite mining industry and the expanding tourist trade caused a boom in the economy of Jamaica.[3] For Trinidad, affluence (by West Indian standards) was nothing new, but her position also greatly changed for the better.[4] Oil production more than doubled and secondary industries were establishing themselves even before active government promotion began. More important perhaps than this economic improvement was the fact that toward the end of the period the community began to acquire a greater self-respect, self-confidence, unity, and sense of purpose under the government of the newly formed People's National Movement led by Eric Williams.

Thus these two communities, Jamaica and Trinidad, under competent local leadership, saw the first evidences of self-sustaining economic growth, and soon each began to feel a new confidence in its own ability to achieve a separate independence. Jamaican nationalism, dormant since 1947, awoke and became a force once more, directing itself now no longer against Britain, but against the new menace that had arisen in the dim and distant regions of the eastern Caribbean—the Federal Government. Trinidadian nationalism, on the other hand, newly aroused by the PNM on the eve of federation, deliberately allied itself with West Indianism and federation; and in the controversial debates of the Intergovernmental Conferences between 1959 and 1961 Trinidad consistently advocated a strong federal center from the start, as against the insistence of Jamaica

3. For example, the Gross Domestic Product in Jamaica rose from £ 120 million (U. S. $336 million) in 1954 to £ 208 million (U. S. $582.4 million) in 1959, an increase of 73 percent.

4. From 1954 to 1959, the Gross Domestic Product in Trinidad rose from W. I. $404 million (U. S. $235.7 million) to W. I. $775 million (U. S. $452 million), an increase of 92 percent.

[43]

that for the next decade or so the Federal Government should not have power to intervene in matters affecting the economic development of the Units.

Trinidad, unlike Jamaica, had long been used to being one of the West Indian islands, and had been imbued with West Indian sentiment through long intercourse with her neighbors in many fields and at all levels. The fact that the federal capital was situated in Trinidad was an influential factor tending to encourage her sympathetic attitude toward the federal point of view. But Trinidadian nationalism had become strong and was growing stronger; and after Jamaican nationalism had seized the opportunity thrown to it and plucked Jamaica from the Federation, Trinidadian nationalism, flushed with the great victory of the PNM in the recent Trinidad elections, asserted itself and followed suit. The fact that Trinidad, in announcing her withdrawal from the federal system, at the same time issued an invitation to all or any of the islands in the eastern group to join the unitary state of Trinidad and Tobago is a sign that here West Indian sentiment has been suppressed but not uprooted. Even in the Jamaican case, in the light of the historical and other obstacles, the determined West Indian optimist may regard the more than 46 percent vote in favor of Jamaica's remaining in the West Indian political system as a sign of considerable progress in the acceptance of the West Indian idea.

CHAPTER 4

FACTORS AT WORK IN THE PROCESS OF FEDERAL UNION

I.

K. C. Wheare, writing in the early 1940's with his eye on the modern federations then in being (in particular the United States, Canada, Switzerland, and Australia), observed that where the desire for a federal union had arisen the following factors had been present in every case:

(1) "a sense of military insecurity and the consequent need for common defence";

(2) "a desire to be independent of foreign powers and a realisation that only through union could independence be secured";

(3) "a hope of economic advantage from union";

(4) "some political association of the communities concerned prior to the federal union, either in a loose confederation, as with the American states or the Swiss cantons, or as parts of the same Empire, as with the Canadian and Australian colonies";

(5) "geographical neighbourhood";

(6) "similarity of political institutions."[1]

Wheare concluded that it was unlikely that countries would desire federal union unless these factors or most of them were present. Recent West Indian experience suggests a footnote to Wheare.

It will be observed that Wheare's six factors fall readily

1. K. C. Wheare, *Federal Government* (Oxford: Oxford University Press, 1946), p. 37.

into two classes which may be described as (a) predisposing conditions and (b) inducements. Previous political association, geographical neighborhood, and similarity of political institutions may properly be described as predisposing conditions; while the sense of need for common defense, the desire for independence, and the hope of economic advantage are clearly in the class of inducements. This distinction between "predisposing conditions" and "inducements" is relevant when we are paying attention to the actual process of creating a federal union out of previously separate units, especially where the process has been as long drawn out and agonizing as in the West Indian case; and on reflection I conclude that it is the inducements that are the deciding factors. It seems unlikely that countries will desire union unless at least one of the inducements is present, and present in sufficient strength to overcome the natural reluctance on the part of communities, which have long been accustomed to leading a separate existence and making decisions independently of their neighbors, to relinquish to a central authority any part of their freedom of decision.

II.

Before pursuing this point further, let us see how far Wheare's factors were present in the West Indian case. Let us begin with the *predisposing conditions,* and take the last one first—*similarity of political institutions.* This condition applies. Even the Crown Colony constitutions, which before the war were to be found in every territory except Barbados, were parliamentary in type; and the post-war constitutions, like the traditional Barbados one, are modeled on the British parliamentary system.

The next condition is *geographical neighborhood.* This is a concept that cannot be defined precisely. It has something to do with distance, and something to do with association. The question whether it is sea or land, mountain or valley that separates the neighbors is also relevant. It seems safe to say that, if the West Indian communities had been adjacent on a continuous land mass, the idea of federation as the method of unifying them would never have occurred. Three million people on eight thousand square miles of land (see Appendix B) is not a very big country; and had it not been for separation by sea, it is

[46]

unlikely that the communities would have developed separate personalities to the degree that would have made the federal solution the appropriate one. But even as things are, the important fact is that distance is not absolute, but relative to other factors—especially means of communication. Thus the advent of air travel some twenty years ago put Jamaica for the first time within reach of the eastern Caribbean.[2] The condition of geographical neighborhood may be said to have been present during this recent period, though hardly before.

The third of the predisposing conditions is *previous political association*. This condition is literally applicable to the West Indian case because of Wheare's qualification, "as parts of the same Empire." Political association between the islands themselves existed only in the Leeward and Windward Islands, and even in them only to a modest degree. There was a Legislative Council for the Leeward Islands, but the fact that it was composed of delegates from the Legislative Councils of the separate islands of Antigua, St. Kitts-Nevis-Anguilla, and Montserrat condemned it to ineffectiveness. In the Windward Islands there was only the slight extent of association implied in the fact that Grenada, St. Lucia, St. Vincent, and Dominica shared one Governor.

Before the Federal Government of the West Indies came into operation, there was never a center of authority or government for the whole of the West Indies, as Lagos was for Nigeria and Delhi for India. The nearest thing to it was the Regional Economic Committee (REC) which was instituted in 1951 and went out of existence shortly after the signing of the agreement to federate. It was composed of representatives of the governments of all the territories and maintained a secretariat in Barbados at the headquarters of the regional Development and Welfare Organization. But the Regional Economic Committee, as its name implies, dealt with a limited range of problems and it had no decision making power.

2. In the 1920's traffic between Jamaica and the eastern Caribbean was chiefly via Great Britain. For this reason the bishops of the Province of the West Indies found it more convenient to meet with their archbishop in London or New York than in the West Indies.

The three predisposing conditions, then, are present—if not always in great strength.

When we come to the *inducements* (which, I am suggesting, are the operative factors), we find that they are present intermittently, weakly, or not at all. If we arrange them in ascending order of importance for unification, the first is the *hope of economic advantage* from union. This hope was shared by all the islands in 1947, but by 1958 only the smaller islands firmly retained it. In the case of Jamaica, a new-found acquaintance with the theory and practice of generating economic development and an accession of unwonted income in comparatively large quantities from the recently inaugurated bauxite mining operations had raised an important question for her leaders. They wondered whether it was any longer to her advantage to develop as part of the federal system, with all that implied in respect of ceding power to the Federal Government, rather than to develop as a separate country in complete control of her own affairs.

Trinidad, richer and longer involved in the actual process of economic modernization, had the same grounds as Jamaica for doubting whether the economic advantage to be achieved for herself by federal union was greater than could be achieved without. But Trinidad was not yet fully moved by the island nationalism that was even then gathering force and, on the other hand, by reason of long association and intercourse with the neighboring islands, she was more deeply committed than Jamaica to the goal of West Indian nationhood. She therefore held firmly to the view—the logical one if there was to be national planning and if the nation was to be the West Indies—that what was required was strong central direction and coordination of all economic development in the interest of the West Indian nation.

There was, as we have seen, considerable discussion, at the series of meetings between representatives of the West Indian governments from 1959 to 1961, of the question whether the vital matter of economic development should be withheld from the power of the Federal Government for the first decade or so after independence. Jamaica unequivocally took the position that it should be so withheld; and it is interesting to note that in the final discussion of this topic[3] a number of the smaller islands supported the proposals that embodied the Jamaican view. When the vote was taken, only the Federal Government and the Government of Grenada recorded their votes against them, though Trinidad made it clear that she gave up her stand for the Federation's entering upon independence with a strong federal center, not on principle, but out of recognition of the special economic and social problems of Jamaica as these had been represented by the Jamaican delegate.[4]

The second inducement is the *desire for independence.* This factor is closely associated in practice with the previous one, since economic viability and independence are interconnected. The desire to be independent of the Colonial Office was still general in 1958, but it was considerably weakened in some quarters by the achievement of complete or almost complete internal self-government. Each island now enjoyed what to the political leaders of small countries must seem in their inmost hearts an almost ideal situation—one in which most of the pleasures of freedom are enjoyed, with far fewer of the corresponding responsibilities. The example of Puerto Rico close by, with its profitable and free association with the United States, excited a degree of envy in the breasts of some, and tended to raise the question whether there was necessarily any advantage in independence other than a change of international status. Nevertheless the desire for independence did persist—with, however, an important difference, namely, that the pressure exerted in the direction of independence (the pressure, that is, of nationalism) was no longer in every case a unifying factor. Island nationalism tended to take priority over West Indian nationalism,[5] as we saw in the preceding chapter. The conviction that only through union could independence be secured had grown considerably weaker in some quarters.

As for the third inducement, the *need for common defense,*

3. *West Indies Intergovernmental Conference Report,* May 1961, sec. 157–186.

4. *Ibid.,* sec. 174.

5. This tendency was exhibited even by Montserrat, whose Chief Minister took an independent line with the Federal Government over their right to send official advisers to the island.

[49]

it is doubtful whether this has had much influence on West Indian leaders, or has been much in their thoughts. Long years of unbroken security have induced a facile acceptance of this happy state as though it were a law of nature. When they have thought about the question of defense, West Indians have tended to assume that the military might of Britain and the United States will always be available in time of need at it was during World War II. The need of a defense force for an independent West Indian nation was indeed recognized, and provision for it was made in the federal arrangements. But it is undoubtedly true that the fear of external enemies has not been present as a unifying motive. It is perhaps not to be expected that the sense of insecurity should come into operation before the cold shock of exposure to the realities of actual independence has been experienced.

Jamaica had a slight foretaste of the kind of possible dangers she might be exposed to when, in the middle of 1960, certain incidents occurred that were faintly reminiscent of recent events in the neighboring island of Cuba—only faintly reminiscent, but sufficiently so for the idea to cross the minds of a number of the more thoughtful people, and confirm the previously held opinion of others, that in the light of modern international practice the existence of a Federal Government was perhaps the only defense available to Jamaica against a successful *coup d'état.* A year and a half earlier, on January 14, 1959, S. G. Fletcher, managing director of the *Gleaner,* had written: "A small unit on its own, under self-government, can easily become a dictatorship—witness Dominican Republic, Haiti, Nicaragua, even Cuba. A Federal Government, a Federal Army, and a Federated police force will be a safeguard against local dictatorship in any Unit and an influence in maintaining the rule of law. A Federal dictatorship is hard to visualise in our island-hopping context." Such thoughts may well have entered the mind of the Government in the summer of 1960, but the die was already cast and the risk had to be taken. Only a matter of weeks before, the fatal decision to hold the referendum had been made. Second thoughts, if they did come, came too late.

III.

I suggested earlier that a country about to enter into a federal union is inhibited by a psychological barrier that can be overcome only by a strong motive—that is, by what I called "induce-ments" among the unifying factors that Wheare discerned in the formation of modern federations up to 1945. Among these in-ducements, the need for common defense is at the head of the list. In the order of priority, the desire for independence and the hope of economic advantage are second and third, with a close link between them.

The sense of need for common defense was the chief unifying motive in the creation of the United States of America; in the more recent and perhaps even more remarkable instance of Western Europe, the fear of Russia has been the decisive factor in the initiation of the movement toward integration; fear of the United States of America operated in the unification of Canada; and the fear of German expansionism in the Pacific was a motive in the Australian case. All communities seek first of all survival, then prosperity (which may be variously interpreted). They may compromise about prosperity, but they will never knowingly do so about survival. A community will *sometimes* unite with other communities for the sake of economic advantage or because it is driven by the urge toward independence. Communities will *always* unite if this action seems to be necessary for their survival.

How difficult it is for federal unity to be preserved, even if it is successfully initiated, without the sense of danger, is illustrated not only by the West Indian case but also by the examples of the other postwar federations that have been created out of former empires of European countries. There has been a tendency for their component units to fall apart. This tendency toward disintegration has been more marked in Africa (for example, French West Africa and French Equatorial Africa) than in Asia; and it is relevant to our argument to suggest that the cause of this lies in the fact that the countries concerned in Asia are more directly exposed than those in Africa to the threat of external aggression.

IV.

A further word needs to be said. The process of federal union does not end with the creation of the federal system. Carl Friedrich and others have emphasized that the creation of

[51]

a federal state is not an event but a process, and is therefore subject to the interrelation, cooperation, and exchange, the permanent give and take between the inclusive community and the component communities which is a universal principle of political organization.[6] So it is that in the United States, for example, the widening of the sphere of government in the area of the social services, the centralizing tendency induced by the imperatives of economic stabilization and control, and the requirements of national defense have led, over a period of time, to a change in the relation between the federal government and the state governments. In place of "dualism" there is now "cooperation," in which the states supply the local knowledge and personnel and the center supplies the funds.

Reference to this process may seem to have little relevance to our study of the short-lived West Indian federal union. But since, in the context of West Indian and British constitutional law and practice, the Jamaican referendum of September 19, 1961, must be regarded as gratuitous rather than necessary, it is easy to envisage the continued existence of the federal state as it might have been (and permissible to hope that the historical trend in the direction of larger entities and the forces behind it will bring these small countries together again in the not too distant future).

E. B. Haas, in his reflections on the early progress of the European integration movement, and in particular the Coal and Steel Community, has some interesting and suggestive things to say which are relevant to our present discussion. "Acceptance of a federal scheme," he says, "is facilitated if the participating state units are already fragmented ideologically and socially." He goes on to indicate that the "fragments" he refers to are interest groups. He observes that the pressures of industrial groups —for example, business and labor—tend to spill over into the federal sphere and thereby add to the integrative impulse, since they seek to obtain common benefits by uniting beyond their former national boundaries. Political parties, likewise, tend to fall into the same pattern. Even national governments in the long run bring themselves to defer to federal decisions, lest the

6. C. J. Friedrich, in *Federalism, Mature and Emergent,* ed. A. W. Macmahon (Garden City, N. Y.: Doubleday, 1955).

example of their recalcitrance act as a precedent for other governments.

Haas thinks that an external threat is a helpful but "by no means indispensable" inducement. He notes that "once established the central institution will affect political integration meaningfully only if it is willing to follow policies giving rise to expectations and demands for more or fewer federal measures," thus stimulating the interest group to seek to influence policy. "If the central institution, however, fails to assert itself in any way so as to cause strong positive or negative expectations, its impact on unity will be small. . . ."

He concludes that "the process of community formation is dominated by nationally constituted groups with specific interests and aims, willing and able to adjust their aspirations by turning to supra-national means when this course appears profitable," and that "a larger political community can be developed if the crucial expectations, ideologies and behaviour patterns of certain key groups can be refocused on a new set of central symbols and institutions." He adds a *caveat* to the effect that these generalizations only apply to societies where similar operative factors are to be found, where key groups exist in a sufficiently developed form, with identifiable and competing leadership, and where there is a sufficiently well-established tradition of democracy and constitutionalism.[7]

These conditions exist in the West Indies, though to a degree less advanced than in Western Europe. Over the period since 1947, when the federal arrangements began to be officially discussed, appreciable progress has been made in the integration of Jamaica with the other islands—not at the emotional level of nationalist feeling, but in the practical activities of business[8] and in the unexciting everyday relations for which opportunities have been increasingly provided by the multiplication of areas of active cooperation. Such areas are the common services provided by the Federal Government—the defense forces, the meteorological services, regional shipping, the regional civil

7. E. B. Haas, *The Uniting of Europe* (Stanford: Stanford University Press, 1958), pp. xiii–xiv.

8. Entrepreneurs from Trinidad have begun to invest in Jamaica and vice versa.

aviation authority, and the University (as well the cooperation involved in the management of it, as the common life of the students and staff and the University's relations with the community at the levels of research, consultation and extension work); the cooperation of Unit governments and commodity associations with the Federal Government in the marketing of crops; the regional federation of professional associations, trade unions, sporting organizations, and agricultural, industrial, and commercial associations and groups. Finally, the impact of the Federal Government itself, including the controversies excited by the customs union recommendations, the Federal Land Acquisition Act and the Prime Minister's veiled threat of retroactive taxation, was felt in Jamaica as well as in the other communities by reason of the debate and discussion that these controversies aroused, and the taking up of positions for and against.

Through these means, the fact of federation was beginning to be accepted as a reality even while the Federal Government was being criticized. It is not entirely unreasonable to suppose that if the union had not been broken in the way it was, the process of integration, whose evidences we have just glanced at, would have gone on at an increasing pace.

CHAPTER 5

PROSPECTS FOR THE WEST INDIES

I.

The effects of science and technology upon communications and upon the scale and methods of production and trade have created a world trend in the direction of larger rather than smaller political entities. The West Indies even as a whole is not large; so the break-up of the federal system, along with the consequent persistence of its component units as separate entities, is a paradox. It is not, however, unique; events in parts of Africa have been somewhat similar. By way of explanation I have suggested that what is lacking in these situations is a compelling pressure or inducement of sufficient strength to enable the component units to overcome voluntarily their natural reluctance to accept the subordination to a central authority that political amalgamation entails.

Another part of the explanation may be the fact that the countries in question still continue to look to their former metropolitan countries for the economic and technical assistance they so greatly need if they are to survive and make progress. They do not for the moment see comparable advantages to be derived from association with other similarly dependent countries, while they do see without enthusiasm the loss of a measure of control of their own affairs to a Federal Government that is new and inexperienced and with which they have not yet come to identify themselves. They therefore feel a pull, compounded of habit and advantage, toward the metropolitan country and a certain resistance to the doubtful-seeming attraction of the federal center.

But the possibility should not be ruled out that the West Indian Units may decide to come together once more if and when they all recognize that they need to look to one another for mutual support and assistance, and not only to Britain, the United States, and Canada. In today's circumstances of international interdependence this may be the same thing as saying, if and when it is brought home to them, that the prospects of support and assistance from these larger and wealthier countries will be greater and more certain if they themselves combine.

II.

In the light of our previous discussion, let us now ask the question, "In what way is it likely that the 'trend' and the 'forces' we have been speaking of will operate on these islands to bring them closer together?" The unifying factors present or in prospect would seem to be first, association in and through the common services; second, economic factors, especially outside pressure from powerful trading partners and investors who prefer to deal with one larger rather than a number of smaller entities; and, third, the sense of need for a combined defense.

First, the common services. The Federal Government was responsible for a number of common services, of which the most important was the University. The others included principally defense, the shipping service, the meteorological service, regional control of civil aviation, the West Indies Supreme Court and the promotion of regional and overseas trade and marketing. As mentioned before, the beginnings of joint action in these directions by the West Indian communities and governments belong to the period during and immediately after World War II. The Regional Economic Committee, which acted as coordinator of these activities at the government level in the interval between the agreement in principle at Montego Bay in 1947 and the signing of articles in 1956, was universally admitted to have been a success. The Federal Government also, in spite of the financial difficulties and the political stresses and strains under which it labored, managed to do a useful job in expanding and improving these services. The need for this work to be carried on is recognized by those concerned. Both Jamaica and Trinidad have publicly declared themselves in favor of continuing to support them.[1] The Federal Government had made a start in

1. On Jamaica see Ministry Paper No. 3, Feb. 22, 1960, p. 6 (Annexure). On Trinidad see PNM Independence Resolution, Jan. 27, 1962, part 2; also Eric Williams' "Speech on Independence," published as a pamphlet by the PNM (Port-of-Spain, 1962), p. 32.

the training and equipping of a West Indian defense force and in the training of a diplomatic service. But the indications are that Jamaica and Trinidad regard these as no longer coming within the category of common services.

The second unifying factor is the pressure from powerful trading partners and foreign investors. It seems reasonable to suppose that the existence of long established joint arrangements for trade and marketing between the West Indies and larger and more powerful countries, for the most part in respect of commodities difficult to sell in world markets, will have created vested interests as well as a bias in favor of continuing these arrangements. To the extent that this proves to be the case, it seems likely that pressure will be built up in the direction of unifying the economic area. Britain's entry into the European Common Market may also be expected to exert pressure in this direction. In the face of the grave economic dangers to which they are likely to be increasingly exposed (no matter how successful the United Kingdom is in ensuring advantageous relations with Europe for her former colonies), it is difficult to see how the governments of the West Indies will not feel bound to place themselves in the strongest possible position to cope with these dangers. It is assumed for this purpose that an economic unit containing eight thousand square miles and more than three million people will be in a stronger position than any unit of smaller size.

In addition to the likelihood of pressures of this kind from outside, it is possible that the movement toward modernization, as it achieves greater success, may strengthen in Jamaica the motive for customs union. Up to now this motive has been weak, because at the present early stage in the process of establishing new industries the influence of early industrial efforts that rely heavily on protection has been a powerful force in favor of isolation. An increase in the number of efficient mass producing industries may be expected to create pressure for a wider home market.

The third unifying factor is more in prospect than actually present, although in a manner of speaking it has already cast its shadow. Both Trinidad and Jamaica may find themselves with problems of defense or security at an earlier date than most people in those islands expect. There is a possibility of friction between Trinidad and Venezuela over oil rights in the Gulf of Paria, and Jamaica will for some time to come be exposed to the danger of subversion. Thoughtful and far-sighted Jamaicans began to recognize this possibility when the federal controversy arose in 1958 and people began to think seriously about the implications for Jamaica of the federal relationship. I have already quoted the comment made in January 1959 by S. G. Fletcher, managing director of the *Gleaner,* to the effect that a federal government, army, and police force would be a safeguard for Jamaica against local dictatorship and an influence in maintaining the rule of law. The *Gleaner's* editorial of December 31, 1960,[2] reflects the sense of danger current at that time. It referred to Jamaica as being "no longer an isolated island in an archipelago of peace" but "now vulnerable in the sea of contention." The newspaper referred to the fact that "Jamaica is next door to Cuba, the focus of the Communists' entry into the new world," and pointed to the consequent need for a strong and efficient security force:

> Self-government is not a game; it is a ruthless reality and those who govern can easily betray their people if they do not show the realism necessary to deal with the murderers, traitors, insurrectionists, lunatics and sheer nitwits who, given a chance, will upset any government anywhere. . . . We would like to see the government's wisdom in economic affairs matched by a real thoroughness in getting on with the job of the country's security. Because the economic and social progress could disappear overnight if the guardians of the people's peace blink or fall asleep for a moment on their vigil.

A year and a half later a Jamaican writer, commenting on the political situation in Jamaica immediately after the intergovernmental talks in Port-of-Spain and the constitutional con-

2. Written six months after the quite unsuccessful attempt by incompetent would-be revolutionaries, some of whom entered the island illegally, to set up an outlaw center in the hills near Kingston.

ference in London, and shortly before the referendum, was gloomy about the prospects for civil liberties and the rule of law in an independent Jamaica:

> So far, Federation has been discussed either in high-falutin terms of West Indian brotherhood or prosaic ones of hard cash; i.e., will it pay Jamaica to stay in. It is the latter factor which has been most influential here, for that is what wakened Jamaica out of its long sleep. . . . But it is as well to remember that hard cash is not the only criterion and that there are worse things to lose: for instance, personal security, the rule of law, and the right to live one's life in peace and dignity. . . . The innate threat of eventual relapse into disorder and tyranny menaces all the West Indies, but particularly Jamaica and Trinidad and perhaps Jamaica, with its special problems, more than Trinidad. Jamaica's permanent political fever, turbulent populace, economic and racial tensions, make it all but certain that if she were "on her own" as an unfederated but independent state, without external restraints and influences, it would not be long before law and order deteriorated, cynicism and corruption in government supervened, and the way lay open to misrule or tyranny.[3]

It may, of course, be argued that the sense of need for defense in Jamaica and Trinidad may not necessarily lead to a reunification of the islands, but may lead instead to their more permanent separation, since these islands may prefer to make separate defensive alliances with powerful neighbors. Sir Alexander Bustamante, for example, whose party was returned to power in the general election of April 10, 1962, announced on April 12 that he would seek a defense treaty with the United States "to protect us from foreign invasion."[4]

In matters of defense, these islands may be expected to turn increasingly to the United States, as Britain continues to

3. Clinton Parchment, "Federation—Jamaica's Safeguard," *Gleaner*, June 26, 1961.

4. *New York Times*, April 13, 1962.

withdraw from the scene. The argument of defense requirements was used by Britain in inducing New Brunswick to enter the Canadian Federation. The question that arises in the present context is whether the requirements of the United States system of defense for the Caribbean will ever make it necessary to press for the economic and political integration of the region. In such an eventuality the region in question would hardly be limited to the former British colonies. A different and wider pattern of amalgamation would probably take shape.[5] It should be observed, however, that while a defensive treaty with a foreign power would be an appropriate form of protection for Jamaica against the danger of a foreign invasion, a federal relationship with a central government would be more effective insurance against a sudden and successful *coup d'état* organized from within.

Now that we have taken a look at the unifying factors that we hope will exist, it may be well to remind ourselves that there will be a new factor operating in the opposite direction. We must face the fact that the glamour of international recognition at the United Nations and in foreign capitals, and participation in international activities as an independent nation, are bound to create vested interests in the continued separate existence of every independent nation.

III.

Our discussions have been dominated by Jamaica and Trinidad—inevitably, because they are by far the largest islands and have therefore played the principal roles in the federal tragedy. But they do not constitute the immediate problem. Jamaica's independence date is August 6, 1962, and Trinidad's is August 31, 1962. If we take the optimistic view we can say that these two islands have already shown by their postwar development that with a reasonable amount of luck they are capable of achiev-

5. Eric Williams and the PNM in Trinidad have recently accepted as policy an idea the West Indians have sometimes discussed as a distant prospect, namely, that of establishing a common economic community embracing the entire Caribbean area. The party's Independence Resolution of Jan. 27, 1962, declares "the willingness of Trinidad and Tobago to associate with all the peoples of the Caribbean in a Caribbean Economic Community and to take such actions as may be necessary for the achievement of this objective." See also Williams' "Speech on Independence," p. 22.

ing self-sustaining economic growth. For the smaller islands, however, some form of unification seems to be essential—to a lesser extent for Barbados than for the Windwards and Leewards —and this is an immediate problem.

Barbados has always paid her way and would presumably continue to do so if she could be assured of a continuing market for her two chief exports—sugar and people. If she maintains the efficiency of her sugar production and the quality of her educational system, the size of the market she requires is not too big to be available indefinitely, given a reasonable amount of good will on the part of her traditional neighbors and trading partners. With her climate, her amenities and public services,[6] her traditions and her educated population, she should continue to attract industrial investment in a small way and slowly, but steadily and cumulatively. As an independent nation, if it came to that, she would not be either the smallest or the most negligible of the members of the United Nations organization.

The Windward and Leeward Islands constitute an administrative problem which must be solved by some form of unification. It would seem that they have much to gain by joining together to share administrative and technical services (both to reduce their cost and to improve their quality). The chances of successfully achieving such unification of services are better today with modern means of communication than they ever have been. The main obstacle is likely to be the resistance of local vested interests in each island; still, the shock inflicted by the break-up of the Federation may have provided the psychological preparation required for removing this obstacle.

Their chances of attracting manufacturing industries are far less than those of Trinidad or Jamaica or Barbados. They could grow more food than they do at present, and supply a much greater part of their own needs as well as provide a surplus for export to Barbados and Trinidad, with either of which two islands there would be advantages in their joining. From the point of view of their economic development, Trinidad has the attractions of wealth and size. But the islands balk at the

6, "Barbados possesses public utilities and services comparable to those of the most highly developed countries of the world." From "Survey of Barbados," *The Times Weekly Review* (London), Feb. 22, 1962.

[61]

prospect of losing their identity in a unitary state of Trinidad and Tobago, which is the only possibility at present offered to them by Trinidad.[7] The prospect of uniting with Barbados appears to be politically more attractive, and during the last week of February 1962, the Heads of the Governments of Barbados, the Leeward Islands, and the Windward Islands met in Barbados and agreed on constitutional and financial proposals for the unification of these eight islands which they have submitted to the Secretary of State for the Colonies.

IV.

Epilogue by a West Indian

Our common origins and associations have created and are in process of molding a people. This is shown in our way of life, our food and drink, our sport, our recreations, our arts. Our poets, novelists, playwrights, dancers, painters, and sculptors are recognizably West Indian. The West Indian Festival of Arts in Port-of-Spain in 1958 on the occasion of the opening of the Federal Parliament was a revelation in this respect. Dancing especially contributed to the impression of unity amid variety. Dancers from Jamaica, Trinidad, Grenada, Carriacou, and Dominica were richly diverse, yet in some fundamental way similar, in their contributions. The University College of the West Indies has already put out some ten graduating classes of West Indians, who have delighted to discover their mutual likenesses while learning to accept their provincial differences.

Our differences are real. But we are not dismayed by them. Our provincial loyalties are not to be despised; loyalty must begin somewhere. Difference and diversity can enrich and stimulate.

Federation is a challenge to move into a new dimension of life and thought, and to achieve a fuller and freer life as members of a wider community. The challenge has been let go, partly by

7. Cf. the PNM Independence Resolution of Jan. 27, 1962, part I: "That Trinidad and Tobago reject unequivocally any participation in the proposed Federation of the Eastern Caribbean and proceed forthwith to National Independence, *without prejudice to the future association in a unitary State of the People of Trinidad and Tobago with any Territory of the Eastern Caribbean whose people may so desire,* and on terms to be mutually agreed, but in any case providing for the maximum possible degree of local government" *(italics added).*

reason of human error, partly because of what Mr. Manley aptly described in his speech at the Montego Bay Conference as "the vested interest of ambition in power." It may well be that the historian of the future will look back on the period of the next few years as being necessary to cure us of some of our sentimentality and some of our immaturity, so that when we next come together we shall do so with greater respect for one another and a sounder understanding of what each and all of us will be able to contribute to the common good. If this should come about, as I hope and believe it will, the union we shall create will be a healthier and more propitious one.

APPENDIX A
DISTURBANCES OF THE 1930's

This appendix consists of an extract from the report of the Royal Commission of 1938–39, ch. 10, par. 17, as follows:

One of the outstanding phenomena in the history of the West Indies during the last few years is the occurrence of public disorders of such magnitude as to have led in all except three cases to the appointment of a Commission to investigate the causes and character of the outbreak. A list of these disturbances in order of date is given below:

May–July, 1934 . . . . . Disturbances on sugar estates in Trinidad.

January, 1935 . . . . . . Disturbances in St. Kitts.

May, 1935 . . . . Strike of wharf labour at Falmouth, Jamaica, followed by disturbances.

September–October, 1935 . . Disturbances at various estates in British Guiana.

October, 1935 . . . . . . Rioting in Kingstown and Camden Park, St. Vincent.

June, 1937 . . . . General disturbances in Trinidad.

July, 1937 . . . . Disturbances in Barbados.

May, 1938 . . . . Disturbances on the Frome Estate, Jamaica.

May–June, 1938 . . . . . General disturbances in Jamaica.

February, 1939 . . . . . . Disturbances at Leonora Plantation and neighbouring areas in British Guiana.

AREA AND POPULATION OF THE
WEST INDIES, 1960

	Area (sq. miles)	Population (1960 census)	Population per sq. mile
Jamaica	4,411	1,606,500	364
Cayman Islands	100	7,600	—
Turks and Caicos Islands .	166	5,700	—
Trinidad and Tobago . . .	1,980	825,700	417
Barbados	166	232,100	1,398
Windward Islands			
Grenada	133	88,600	666
St. Lucia	238	86,200	362
St. Vincent	150	80,000	533
Dominica	305	59,500	195
Leeward Islands			
Antigua	171	54,400	318
St. Kitts-Nevis-Anguilla .	153	56,600	370
Montserrat	32	12,200	381
Total	8,005	3,115,100	

APPENDIX C

GROSS DOMESTIC PRODUCT PER HEAD
IN FOUR ISLANDS, 1958

	W. I. dollars	U. S. dollars
Trinidad	851	496
Jamaica	596	348
Barbados	474	277
Antigua	333	194

Source: C. O'Loughlin, in *Social and Economic Studies*, University College of the West Indies, September 1961, p. 238.